A
Computer Model
of Skill Acquisition

ELSEVIER COMPUTER SCIENCE LIBRARY

Operating and Programming Systems Series
Peter J. Denning, Editor

1. *Halstead* A Laboratory Manual for Compiler and Operating System Implementation
Spirn Program Behavior: Models and Measurement (in prep.)

Programming Languages Series
Thomas E. Cheatham, Editor

1. *Heindel and Roberto* LANG-PAK—An Interactive Language Design System
2. *Wulf et al* The Design of an Optimizing Compiler
Cleaveland and Uzgalis Grammars for Programming Languages (in prep.)
Hecht Global Code Improvement (in prep.)
Maurer The Programmer's Introduction to SNOBOL (in prep.)

Theory of Computation Series
Patrick C. Fischer, Editor

1. *Borodin and Munro* The Computational Complexity of Algebraic and Numeric Problems

Computer Design and Architecture Series
Edward J. McCluskey, Editor

Salisbury Microprogrammable Computer Architectures (in prep.)

Artificial Intelligence Series
Nils J. Nilsson, Editor

1. *Sussman* A Computer Model of Skill Acquisition

A
Computer Model
of Skill Acquisition

Gerald Jay Sussman

Artificial Intelligence Laboratory, Massachusetts Institute of Technology

American Elsevier Publishing Company, Inc.

New York   London   Amsterdam

AMERICAN ELSEVIER PUBLISHING COMPANY, INC.
52 Vanderbilt Avenue, New York, N.Y. 10017

ELSEVIER PUBLISHING COMPANY
335 Jan Van Galenstraat, P.O. Box 211
Amsterdam, The Netherlands

ISBN 0-444-00159-X (Paperbound Edition)
ISBN 0-444-00163-8 (Hardbound Edition)

MATH

Library of Congress Cataloging in Publication Data

Sussman, Gerald Jay.
  A computer model of skill acquisition.

  (Elsevier computer science library: Artifiicial
intelligence series; 1)
  Bibliography: p.
  1. Electronic data processing—Problem solving.
2. Artificial intelligence. I. Title.
QA63.S87   001.53'5   74-30964
ISBN 0-444-00163-8
ISBN 0-444-00159-X pbk.

SD
12/2/75

Manufactured in the United States of America.

To
The Maharal of Prague
(Rabbi Judah Low ben Bezalel c. 1525-1609)
who noticed that
"And God created man in His own image"
is recursive.

Contents

Foreword

Artificial Intelligence can be defined in a narrow sense as the enterprise of endowing machines with certain abilities. In a wider sense it means re-thinking cognitive problems, philosophical and psychological, with the help of a powerful and growing battery of new theoretical constructs which have emerged from the science and practice of modern computation. The knowledge thereby obtained is applicable to machines and to people much in the same (non-reductionist) way as the laws of aerodynamics scarcely care whether they are applied to understanding the flight of birds or to the design of airplanes.

Sussman's work is a prototypical example of Artificial Intelligence in the wider senses and should be quite as interesting to psychologists as to computer scientists. I'd like to mention two general features, whose balance makes many of us see HACKER, the program described in this monograph, as a remarkably elegant example of this direction of work, and also one very specific feature, which defines a more precisely identifiable theoretical assertion made by Sussman's thesis. The first of the general features is a drive to make computer languages more powerful and expressive, which is seen in his papers (with Drew McDermott) on CONNIVER as well as throughout the present monograph. The second general feature is Sussman's pursuit of the goal followed by psychologists like Titchener, Bartlett, and Wertheimer of capturing in formal scientific description the mental processes of which we are all vaguely aware in our own heads. These two features interact strongly. Sussman's sense of the direction of evolution of computer languages is informed by his perception of his own intellectual processes and, conversely, his ability to sharpen this perception is enhanced by his possession of a better elaborated descriptive apparatus than was available to Bartlett or Wertheimer.

The image of Artificial Intelligence as a "new mentalism" might seem paradoxical to many observers who would expect it to be more akin to "behavioristic" or "mechanistic" trends in psychology. It might also seem to be a dangerously "subjective" basis for developing

ix

theories about how to build intelligent machines. My purpose here is not to settle such doubts, but to draw attention through them to the fact that Sussman's monograph, if discussed more than superficially, rapidly engages fundamental questions. This makes it an excellent seminar text for students in psychology or in computer science and especially for those who see emerging out of the interaction of these disciplines a new Kuhnian paradigm for cognitive theory.

Such discussion could easily head back to the armchair of the speculative philosopher. It can be restrained from doing so by a device, very well illustrated in Sussman's works, which is proving to be one of the more powerful and fruitful ideas of recent trends in Artificial Intelligence. This device consists of studying the operation of intelligence within "mini-worlds" chosen in terms of the current state of the art so as to be sufficiently simple to permit very thorough understanding and sufficiently structured to allow interesting phenomena to show themselves. The best known example, and the one Sussman modifies for his own purposes, is the "blocks world," which proved so useful to the development of the ideas of Patrick Winston, the student of scene analysis, and Terry Winograd. Other examples are the "Turtle World," which has been the context for a recent thesis by Ira Goldstein which in many ways is complementary to Sussman's, and an "electronics world" which is beginning to spawn promising results. Within his well defined mini-world, in which a simple robot acquires skills relevant to stacking blocks, Sussman is able to ask a series of questions which, I think, best mark the radical originality of Artificial Intelligence with respect to the tradition of psychological thinking about learning. The initial question in very informal terms is this: What kind of knowledge about the process of learning would help a learner learn? But only trivial answers can be found to questions stated so generally. You can't (significantly) think about thinking without thinking about somebody thinking about something! In this case the somebody is the robot defined in terms of an internal computational structure, and the something is a task environment defined in terms of the blocks world. So the more finely textured questions are about how to coordinate the definition of kinds of knowledge, the design of a computational structure, and the understanding of the task environment in such a way that the process of learning comes into focus as no longer mysteriously intangible, but instead clear, computationally simple and in tune with what we know about learning from observation of ourselves and from experiments in the laboratory.

The fundamental novelty is the emergence of an epistemological theory of learning. The suggestion is that learning, particularly the acquisition of apparently complex skills, has appeared exaggeratedly mysterious just as the achievement of a navigator would if we observed his ability to guide the ship across oceans to a precise destination but were ignorant of the fact that his knowledge of the stars enabled him quite simply to read his course. What kind of knowledge does a learner use to steer his course to competence? The deep value of HACKER is that it gives us an example; imperfect and incomplete as a theory, but with a startlingly elegant simplicity that recalls, for me, such other simple examples as Galileo's body in natural fall. Those who wish to measure the progress of Artificial Intelligence by the I.Q. of operational programs could do well to reflect on the futility of Galileo wasting time on a falling stone when all the heavens need explanation.

I conclude by raising two themes for reflection, the first a good seminar topic, the second more suited for moments of quiet contemplation.

It may be objected that HACKER is a weak model of learning because the system knows so much in advance. There is an appearance of circularity in the assertion that learning is really quite simple if you have already learned a lot. The theme for reflection is that a host of ideas in computer science — "recursion" and "boot-strap" for example — take the viciousness out of such circles in the spirit of what philosophers sought to do with too vague, too untechnical concepts such as "dialectical."

The theme for quieter reflection is the proposition at the head of Sussman's text: " 'God created man in his own image' is recursive." And so Sussman, in turn, created HACKER in his own image. But this does suggest another question which should not be forgotten any more than it should be allowed to interfere with pursuing a promising line of research. The question is whether Sussman, in creating HACKER in his image, also, to some extent, recreated himself in HACKER's image?

Seymour Papert
Artificial Intelligence Laboratory
Massachusetts Institute of Technology

Preface

How much time has each of us spent tracking down some "bug" in a computer program, an electrical instrument, or a mathematical proof? At best, we feel that a bug is a nuisance; at worst it is a disaster. This monograph presents a new theory of the nature of intellectual skills and how they are acquired. It takes the point of view that bugs are often manifestations of powerful strategies of creative thinking—that creating and fixing bugs are necessary steps in the normal process of adapting new knowledge for the solution of new problems. I call this new theory "Problem Solving by Debugging Almost-Right Plans". This cognitive theory is exhibited as the structure of a computer program which solves problems and improves with practice.

The cognitive theory should be relevant to those who have a theoretical interest in the processes of learning and problem solving, including cognitive psychologists, philosophers, and educational theorists. It illustrates the synthetic, Artificial Intelligence approach to cognitive studies. In addition, computer scientists, especially those involved in Automatic Programming, will find the techniques used to be novel and illuminating. I think that I present material which clarifies aspects of the programming process, including some insights into the natures of plans, comments, and bugs.

Gerald Jay Sussman
Artificial Intelligence Laboratory
Massachusetts Institute of Technology

Acknowledgements

I would like to express my thanks to all of the people who aided and encouraged this work:

to Seymour A. Papert, who asked deep and thought-provoking questions;

to Marvin L. Minsky, who made more contributions than I can remember, and who, with Seymour Papert, created the intellectual environment in which this kind of work is possible,

to Patrick H. Winston, whose criticism and encouragement were very valuable;

to Terry Winograd, Drew V. McDermott, Ira Goldstein, and Allen L. Brown, with whom I had many long discussions and who asked just the right questions at the right times;

to Carl Hewitt, with whom I have had many inspiring arguments;

to Richard Greenblatt, who got me started on this work;

to Bill Gosper, whose philosophical outlook on the nature of the art and science of programming has had a profound influence on my own outlook;

to Joel Moses, whom I cannot bully;

and to Julie Sussman, who contributed to the technical content, presentation, and preparation of this document, as well as to the sanity of the author.

Gerald Jay Sussman

Publisher's Note

Camera-ready copy for this book was formatted by TJ6, test justifier created by the staff of the MIT-Artificial Intelligence Laboratory. It was set in 30VR and 25FG by the XGP (Xerox Graphic Printer) at the Laboratory. The XGP is serviced by a DEC PDP-11 connected to a DEC PDP-10 computer running ITS (the Incompatible Time Sharing System developed by staff of the Artificial Intelligence Laboratory).

The system described above has allowed American Elsevier to bypass the usual typesetting procedures, thereby greatly accelerating the publishing process. We are indebted to Dr. Sussman for arranging for American Elsevier to share in this new and developing text-editing technology.

I. Introduction

What is a skill? We say that a plumber is skilled at plumbing, an engineer is skilled at design. Just what do we mean? One dictionary [Note 1] says:

"The ability to use one's knowledge effectively and readily in execution or performance"

"A learned power of doing a thing competently"

An important property of a skill is <u>effectiveness</u>. It wouldn't be enough to memorize all of the facts in the plumber's handbook, even if that could be done. The knowledge would not then be in an effective, usable form. One becomes skilled at plumbing by practice. Without practice it doesn't all hang together. When faced with a problem, a novice attacks it slowly and awkwardly, painfully having to reason out each step, and often making expensive and time-consuming mistakes.

Thus the skill, plumbing, is more than just the information in the plumber's handbook; it is the unwritten knowledge derived from practice which ties the written knowledge together, making it usable.

Just what is this unwritten knowledge? How is a skilled person different from a knowledgeable, unskilled one?

What is the process by which a person develops a skill through practice?

The research reported in this document is an attempt to provide these questions with precise, mechanistic answers by the construction of a computational performance model, a computer program which exhibits behavior identifiable with skill acquisition. The computer program [Note 2] is HACKER, a problem solver whose performance improves with practice.

1

A theory of problem solving

A human problem solver first tries to classify his problem into a subclass for which he knows a solution method. If he can, he applies that method. If he cannot, he must construct a new method by applying some more general problem-solving techniques to his knowledge of the domain. In constructing the new method, he is careful to avoid certain pitfalls he has previously encountered and he may use methods previously constructed to solve subproblems of the given problem. The new method is remembered so that it can be used to solve similar problems in the future. If any method, new or old, fails on a problem for which it is expected to work, the failure is examined and analyzed. As a result, the method may be modified to accommodate the new problem. Often the analysis of the failure can also be abstracted and classified, to be remembered as a pitfall to avoid in the future when constructing new methods.

How HACKER embodies this theory

HACKER, when attacking a problem (in the Blocks World [Note 3]), first checks to see if he has a program in his Answer Library whose pattern of applicability matches the problem statement. If so, he runs that program. If not, he must write a new program, using some general knowledge of programming techniques applied to his knowledge of the Blocks World. The new program is checked for certain bugs which he has previously encountered. He may use subroutines previously constructed to solve subproblems of the given problem. The new program is stored in the Answer Library, indexed by an applicability pattern derived from the statement of the problem for which it was written, so that it can be used to solve similar problems in the future. If any program, new or old, manifests a bug when it is applied to a problem which matches its pattern of applicability, general debugging knowledge is used to classify the mode of failure. As a result, the program is patched to work in the new case. Often the bug itself can be generalized and remembered, to be avoided in the future when constructing new programs.

I consider the previous parallelism truly fundamental. I often wax anthropomorphic because I believe that HACKER represents how people use knowledge to do and learn. I refer to HACKER as "he" and say such things as "he knows" or "he notices". In these statements I am not trying to imply that the detailed mechanisms in HACKER reflect analogous mechanisms in people, but rather that the development of HACKER was guided by introspection on my own problem-solving behavior along the lines of this parallelism.

A theory of skill

From this point of view a skill is a set of answer procedures, each indexed by a description of the problem types for which it is appropriate, along with a set of pitfalls to avoid when it is necessary to construct a new answer procedure. A skill is acquired by the construction of such a store of "runnable" knowledge -- canned answers to problems -- by "compiling" it from knowledge of the problem domain supplied in a more "intelligible" form -- a form designed more for communication than for use as answers to problems. One becomes skilled in a particular domain by going through a training sequence (apprenticeship) in which one is confronted with a series of increasingly complex problems. The solution to each new problem builds on the skill developed by former problems or points out some modification or generalization required. Thus, a skilled problem solver -- one with an extensive store of runnable knowledge -- should find it easier than a relatively unskilled one to learn to solve a new class of problems. Practice is a process of incremental compilation. In this compilation, knowledge of the particular problem domain is combined with more general knowledge about construction and debugging of procedures. The unwritten knowledge which is acquired during practice is that knowledge implicit in the structure of the procedures constructed.

This theory in historical perspective

Problem solving has long been an important issue in Artificial Intelligence. Efficiency and extensibility are among the traditional desiderata for an intelligent problem solver. Historically, problem solvers have fallen naturally into two classes, the "experts" and the "generalists" (though we rarely see the pure form of either class). The experts are optimized for efficiency, the generalists are optimized for extensibility.

The experts are huge, nearly incomprehensible systems which achieve impressive results in a narrow field but are difficult to extend. These systems are written by expert programmers who are also experts in the narrow field for which the program is written. In this class we find DENDRAL <Buchanan 1969>, SHRDLU <Winograd 1971>, Greenblatt's Chess Program <Greenblatt 1967>, and MACSYMA <Bogen 1973>.

The generalists claim generality of applicability and easy extensibility. In this class we find such programs as QA3 <Green 1969a,b> and GPS <Newell 1959>. Typically a generalist applies a uniform procedure which massages a uniformly represented data-base high in declarative and low in imperative content. (The resulting system is usually "complete", in some mathematical sense.) Generalists, however, solve few interesting problems -- for two reasons. First, they are plagued by combinatorial explosion. That is, as the number of data-base facts is increased the performance declines precipitously, even on problems that were solvable in the smaller data-base. Second, the language used to represent knowledge in these systems -- often some form of predicate calculus -- is extremely weak in expressivity, thus making it very difficult to formalize the statements of problems.

> Of course, one might argue that the LISP interpreter is a "uniform procedure which massages uniformly represented data". Thus, since most of the "expert" programs cited are written in LISP, the classification proposed is useless. This misses the point. The data massaged by the LISP interpreter is extremely high in imperative content; indeed, it is a program.

In a sense, the first class of problem solver is too complex to be understood and the second class is too simple to work. The experts have good performance but lack extensibility and the generalists are (perhaps) extensible but have unacceptable performance. How can we combine the desirable features of both classes of problem solver? What are the organizational characteristics of each type of problem solver which contribute to the features desired?

The expert program offers performance. I claim that the performance is due to the procedural representation of knowledge in the expert. For each kind of problem it knows how to solve, a procedure is available which, when interpreted, performs the required manipulations in a directed way. It implicitly "knows" (embedded in the structure of the procedure by the programmer) the correct sequence to perform, including the order of steps and how to avoid or fix destructive interactions between them. It knows to set up for steps that need some conditions to be true, by prior execution of steps which make those conditions true. An expert program is a fully developed "Answer Library".

The generalist program is said to be extensible. It can "easily" assimilate a new fact (though the new fact may be very difficult to express). In a predicate calculus theorem prover like QA3, the data-base consists of a set of <u>true</u> propositions. Knowledge expressed as true propositions is additive in that any new true proposition can be added to the data-base without changing any previously resident proposition. Thus we see that the desirable feature, extensibility, is the result of <u>modularity</u> of the knowledge. Modularity, however, in a less extreme form, means <u>locality</u> of interaction. The feature we desire is that the addition of a new fact to the knowledge base of the system should not require a massive edit of the old information. Knowledge, which is at best additive, should be at worst only locally interactive.

Now, the bind we are in should begin to reveal itself. The efficiency of procedural representation is a result of interaction! Sequencing, setting up, cleaning up, interfacing -- the specifications of the interactions between components of knowledge -- are the very essence of the procedural concept. These provide the sense of direction which the generalist lacks, and thus the performance of the expert, but destroy its modularity. We see that the expert is efficient because it is not modular! No wonder it is difficult to build an efficient and extensible problem solver!

Is the situation hopeless? The HACKER theory tries to avoid the difficulty by storing the knowledge in two different forms: a modular representation, for communication with the user of the problem solver; and a highly interwoven and thus efficient procedural representation for performance. This, of course, requires a method of translation from the modular form to the efficient procedural representation of the knowledge -- that is, a <u>programmer.</u> We see that we need a programmer component in a problem solver which features an extensible knowledge base and efficient performance. The programmer also buys us an extensible command language. After all, we can always ask our programmer to implement a new feature.

Evolutionary programming

It seems that we need an "automatic programmer" [Note 4] as a component of an extensible, efficient problem solver. Many people working on automatic program synthesis expect that a system can be built which will, given a description of the problem to be solved, synthesize a "correct" program [Note 5]. I believe that this approach is a mistake. In real situations the complete specification of a problem is unknown, and what we really see happening is an evolutionary process. The sloppily formulated problem is given to the programmers, who produce a concrete realization. The users then complain about those properties of the realization which do not reflect their needs. This process iterates until the users are satisfied. As the users debug their ideas of what they need, the programmers debug their programs. At no point in this process do either the users or the programmers believe that they fully understand the problem. The iteration usually doesn't terminate because the users continue to evolve new ideas and requirements; so the programs must continually undergo revision due to "bugs" resulting from a misunderstanding or changing of intent. This remains true even in the case where the users are the programmers. Consider how difficult it would be to completely specify an unwritten time-sharing system or compiler. It is monstrously difficult to precisely document even running systems. If this weren't enough, what would we do about a program to understand English or play chess? I believe that the only hope of producing a useful automatic program synthesizer lies in capturing the concept of program evolution. In the evolutionary approach, if a program is to be extended to satisfy a new type of request, the new feature is implemented by building on previously constructed components or subroutines. If an old feature is to be extended to a new situation the code which implements that feature is modified to take into account the newly imposed requirements. If a new piece of knowledge of the problem domain is to be included then the relevant parts of the existing program are dissected out and patched appropriately.

The advantages of such a scheme are manifold. First, there is the efficiency of using old subroutines in new features, so that we don't have to re-invent the wheel for each new vehicle type. Second, when trying to extend an old feature to a new situation, we can try the old feature on the new situation, and see how it fails. This focuses attention on the source of the difficulty, lowering the problem complexity. Thus, we extend existing code to new situations by "debugging" the cause of failure in the new situations. The old code serves as a "plan" for the new code. Not only are we saved from re-inventing the wheel but if new information becomes available which improves the wheel, any program which uses the wheel subroutine will benefit from the improvement.

This scheme has a major disadvantage, as well. At no time does the programmer step back from the local patching and fixing to discover a better organization. This is a major problem which I have not attacked.

Debugging, then, is an important aspect of programming, and evolutionary programming is a natural paradigm for skill acquisition. But debugging is even a bigger and more powerful idea than that. It is important in other kinds of learning, as well. Winston's system [Note 6] for learning descriptions of simple structures suitable for recognition may be viewed as a "theory" debugger. Indeed, Winston's description nets may be considered theories of the structures they describe. A description net has a "bug" if it matches a scene which it shouldn't or vice versa. A bug is fixed by "patching" the description net. Thus, debugging is an important concept in generalization from examples.

The idea of thinking of bugs as important concepts rather than unmentionable pests may seem surprising. But we suspect that isolating and systematizing them may become as important in psychology as classifying interactions has become in physics! (See <Minsky 1970>, section 3.)

II. The Scenario

This chapter is critical to the rest of this document. Its examples are basic to most of the succeeding chapters. The Scenario is an annotated conversation with HACKER, putting him through his paces. In this chapter you are not to expect to understand <u>how</u> HACKER accomplishes his tasks, but rather just <u>what</u> he does accomplish. The succeeding chapters will examine the structure of HACKER and the method by which each step is accomplished.

In the text that follows we will encounter Blocks World scenes, containing a table and various blocks. The primitives for moving objects allow that only one object be moved at a time; thus an object to be moved must have no other objects on it. The movement primitives also require that no two blocks occupy the same place at the same time. If either of these two conditions is violated by a HACKER program, an error condition is the result. All errors transfer control to the debugging routines in HACKER.

In the text a distinction is made between the program-manipulating (writing/debugging) part of HACKER and the programs manipulated. The program manipulated is often called the performance program, and the manipulator is often referred to (somewhat imprecisely) as HACKER.

The Scenario is broken up into Sections in each of which a particular cluster of concepts is being learned. The Sections are subdivided into problems -- the specific situations and commands which HACKER is given. Each scene is set up by the trainer before the problem statement is given, so a problem really is the combination of the scene and the problem statement. Thus HACKER is really being asked: "In this situation how would you ...?". The Scenario is, however, a continuous training sequence, so any general principles learned are retained throughout the rest of the Scenario.

Section 1: Learning about CLEARTOP

Initially, HACKER has no performance programs other than the Blocks World primitives. These, however, are sufficient for the first problem. We set up the scene:

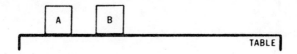

Problem 1.1: (MAKE (ON A B))

Without hesitation, HACKER performs the movement required to achieve the goal. The scene now looks like:

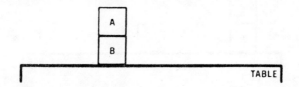

We now introduce a new object, C:

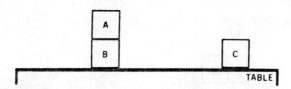

Problem 1.2: (MAKE (ON B C))

This time the performance program fails because it is just a call to a primitive and cannot move B without moving A. The angry primitive delivers an error message. The program manipulator receives the error message and computes a patch to the performance program which, when rerun, now works:

A is put on the TABLE
B is placed on C

The world now looks like:

What has been learned? Consider:

Problem 1.3: (MAKE (ON C A))

Now, with no hesitation, the program resulting from 1.2 puts B on the table, then puts C on A, as required. This results in:

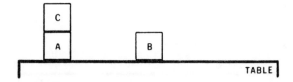

HACKER has learned the skill of putting one object on another when the first has something on it. But that's not all! Consider the new scene:

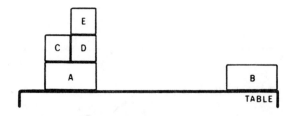

Problem 1.4: (MAKE (ON A B))

The performance program written in 1.2 solves this problem, too, without modification or error! The patch made was sufficiently general:

Steps: Wants to put A on B
        Notices C,D on A
           Puts C on TABLE
           Wants to put D on TABLE
             Notices E on D
                Puts E on TABLE
           Puts D on TABLE
      Puts A on B

This results in:

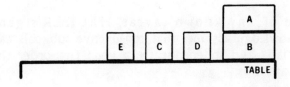

Section 2: Learning that ON-chains must be built from the bottom up.

Consider the scene with 3 blocks -- A, B, and C:

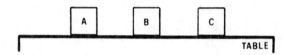

Problem 2.1: (MAKE (AND (ON A B) (ON B C)))

In the absence of any known caveat, HACKER's general programming knowledge assumes that conjunctive subgoals can be achieved sequentially and independently, a good first-order theory. The initial program thus:

>   Step 1: Puts A on B
>   Step 2: Wants to put B on C
>   Notices A on B (as learned in Section 1)
>   Puts A on TABLE

HACKER watches his program run and at this point realizes that there is a bug because Step 2 requires undoing the result of Step 1. HACKER analyzes the bug and, as a result, interchanges the steps, resets the scene, and reruns the program. The second version works: B is put on C, then A on B.

The resulting 3-tower looks like:

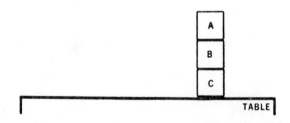

Not only is this bug fixed, the program patched, and this problem solved; but HACKER will not fall into this trap again! The structure of this bug is abstracted and remembered so that:

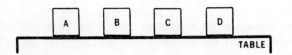

Problem 2.2: (MAKE (AND (ON A B) (ON C D) (ON B C)))

Now HACKER will write a program to build this 4-high tower correctly the first time using the caveat learned in Problem 2.1.

The kind of knowledge learned in this Section is different from the kind learned in Section 1. Whereas in 1 a library routine was improved in generality, in 2 a general principle about Blocks programming was learned.

Section 3: Learning about space allocation.

The primitive block movers can place an object only in a free (empty) place. What do we do about making free space when there isn't any? First consider:

Problem 3.1: (MAKE (ON C B))

This problem is solved immediately because there is space for C on B to the right of A:

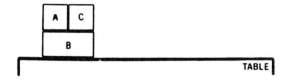

By the way, if there is a choice, the place chooser will always choose the middle of a block to put another on. Suppose we have:

Problem 3.2: (MAKE (ON C B))

This time the performance program fails because there is not enough room on B for C. (NB This is not the same problem as 1.2. In 1.2 the difficulty was that the object to be moved had something on it. Here, there is not enough room on the specified surface to accommodate it.) The angry primitive delivers an error message. The program manipulator receives the error message and computes, from more general knowledge about space, a patch to the performance program, which when rerun now:

Pushes A to the left on B
Puts C on B

This results in:

Suppose we now introduce D:

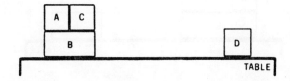

Problem 3.3: (MAKE (ON D B))

The strategy used in 3.2 (call it "compacting") doesn't work here --
there is no place to push A or C. Another strategy, call it "flushing",
is found, which removes objects until there is enough space. The
program is patched so that, if compacting fails to free up enough
space, then flushing is tried. In this case HACKER:

Removes C from B and places it on the TABLE
Puts D on B (where C was)

Now the world looks like:

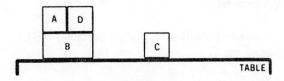

Sometimes we want a problem solved with certain restrictions on
how it is to be solved. Suppose in the current scene we want
HACKER to (MAKE (ON C B)) without allowing him to remove A.
We stipulate this by:

Problem 3.4:
>   (PROTECT (ON A B))
>   (MAKE (ON C B))

HACKER will find, as above, that he cannot push anything over, so
either A or D has to go. But we have forced A to remain, so D is
flushed and C is placed where D was.

HACKER has been trained to try compacting before flushing -- a
non-optimal strategy. Consider the scene:

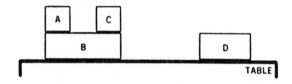

Problem 3.5:
>   (PROTECT (ON C B))
>   (MAKE (ON D B))

HACKER first tries compacting. Only C has open space on its left,
so C is pushed to the middle of B. There is still not enough space
for D on B. Next, HACKER tries flushing A to make space for D.
This cannot help because C is still blocking the middle of B, and C
cannot be flushed. Things are not allowed to get this far, however.
As A is being moved HACKER notices that C suddenly has space
on its left again! So the compactness of the top of B has been
violated by removing A. As in Scenario Section 2, an analysis
indicates that the flushing strategy must be tried before compacting
is tried, if best results are to be expected. The interchange is made
and the new version wins:

>   A is removed from B and placed on the TABLE
>   D is placed on B

This results in:

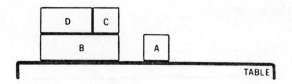

A new scene is needed for problem 3.6:

Problem 3.6:
                (PROTECT (ON C B))
                (MAKE (ON A B))

Since C cannot be flushed, it must be pushed over. But C has D on it, and the physics of the Blocks World requires that D must be removed before C is pushed. (Only one object can be moved at a time.) The initial PUSH program, like the initial ON program, does not consider this. Thus it fails for the same reason that the initial ON program failed in 1.2. HACKER notices the similarity and extracts the patch to ON made in 1.2, subroutinizes it, and replaces the patch by a subroutine call. He also patches PUSH with a call to the same routine. The program now works. It puts D on the table, pushes C over, and puts A down on B, resulting in:

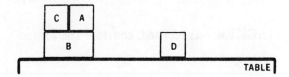

Section 4: Simultaneous space allocation.

We set up the scene:

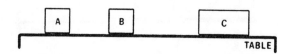

Problem 4.1: (MAKE (AND (ON A C) (ON B C)))

As in problem 2.1, HACKER writes a program which achieves the goals sequentially and independently:

> Step 1: Puts A on middle of C
> Step 2: Puts B on C

>> As learned in 3.2, step 2 must push A rather than remove it because step 1 protected A on C.

HACKER watches his program run and is disturbed by the fact that A was moved twice in the same problem. (This is a piece of "esthetic" knowledge.) From this he learns a new caveat: If more than one object is to be placed on another object, a plan must first be made for where they are to go. A patch is made to implement the fix and the program is rerun.

The result is:

To see what HACKER has learned, consider the scene:

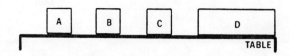

Problem 4.2: (MAKE (AND (ON A D) (ON B D) (ON C D)))

How does HACKER solve this problem? He writes a program which takes into account the interdependence of the subgoals learned in 4.1. The result is a 4-step program:

    Step 1: Plans where to put A, B, and C on D
    Step 2: Places A on D as planned
    Step 3: Places B on D as planned
    Step 4: Places C on D as planned

Now the blocks get placed correctly the first time:

Section 5: Showing Off

This last problem brings together all the skills developed so far:

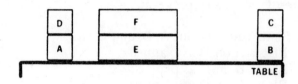

Problem 5:
```
(MAKE (AND (ON D A) (ON B E) (ON A E)
           (ON C E) (ON F D)))
```

HACKER now writes a program which works immediately:

       Step 1: A plan is made for the top of E
                 F is placed on the table
       Step 2: A is placed on E
                 D is placed on the TABLE
       Step 3: B is placed on E
                 C is placed on the TABLE
       Step 4: C is placed on E
       Step 5: D is placed on A
       Step 6: F is placed on D

The result looks like:

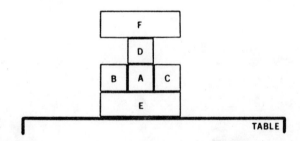

III. Overview of HACKER

Before entering the detailed discussion of how HACKER attacks the Scenario, it is appropriate to stand back and look at his overall structure. In this way we will establish a vocabulary of HACKER's anatomy and some idea of the various functions and interconnections of his parts.

Please turn to Figure 1. In this "flow diagram", HACKER has been broken up into some parts that we will refer to throughout the text. Polygons represent computations and circles represent bodies of knowledge. Control flows along the solid arrows and data flows along the dotted arrows. (Many of the divisions are purely conceptual and do not really represent segmentation of the actual program. The bodies of knowledge are, for example, all uniformly represented as items and methods in a CONNIVER data-base [Note 7]. The diagram is incomplete in that only major paths are shown.)

Problem statements

HACKER accepts commands, i.e., problems to be solved, from the user. A problem is stated to HACKER as a simple s-expression pattern, such as (MAKE (ON B C)) (as in Scenario problem 1.2). The pattern does not completely specify the final state desired, it only specifies a <u>kernel</u> of the problem to be solved, leaving the problem to be further specified by "reasonable" completion. For example, in problem 1.2 we give no indication of what is to be done with block A (initially on B). It is up to HACKER to decide to put A on the TABLE -- we do not particularly care where it is in the goal state. If HACKER found it convenient, he might leave A where it started out, on B. What is the convenient completion of a problem statement depends upon what methods are available to attain the kernel goal, or what methods are retrieved to build and debug an answer if there is not one available.

21

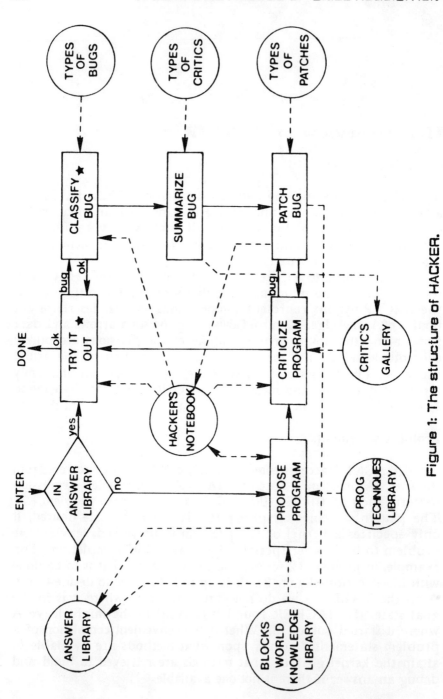

Figure 1: The structure of HACKER.

The Answer Library

Given such a problem statement, HACKER asks himself: "Do I know how to solve problems of this general kind?". That is: Is the problem, as stated, an example of a generalized problem for which a generalized method of solution is known? Specifically, he checks the Answer Library for a program whose pattern of applicability matches the problem statement (has the problem as a substitution instance). The patterns for methods are simple s-expressions which contain variables. This kind of pattern-directed procedure invocation has been a useful tool of Artificial Intelligence research (see [Note 7]). Thus, for example, the program:

```
(TO (MAKE (ON a b))
    step 1
    step 2
    step 3
    ...)
```

would match the problem statement. Here we see a convention used in this document. Pattern-matching syntax is exceedingly complex (for good reasons). However, the fine points of pattern matching are usually irrelevant to the essential ideas displayed. In this document, precision will be sacrificed for readability wherever possible, by simplifying the pattern-matching syntax so that variables will be distinguished from constants by giving them lower-case names. Variable instances which are syntactically distinguished in the real HACKER only because of some uninteresting subtlety will appear here identically. For more complete discussions of pattern matching see [Note 8]. The pattern languages available are rather poor in expressiveness. It is difficult to encode complex requirements elegantly. This limitation of HACKER will improve with better pattern languages.

Note that the atoms MAKE, ON, A, and B are all just abstract pattern symbols. They have no *a priori* meaning to the HACKER-structure, but are defined by their use in the various knowledge bodies. The reader should be able to infer their meanings from context. We will meet other symbols which do have *a priori* meaning. TO, for example, is the definition syntax for an Answer. Others will be explained as they appear.

Trying the answer

Suppose that an appropriate program is found in the Answer Library. It is then run (interpreted step by step). The running of an answer may cause subproblems to be generated, initiating a recursive call to HACKER (not shown in the figure; boxes which can initiate such recursive calls are marked with a star). If the program is successfully executed, HACKER returns control to the user. The user can then supply another problem, or if he is unhappy with the result, he can tell HACKER to restore the state (of HACKER and his world) to the one prevailing before the last command was executed, and rerun the last problem in CAREFUL mode -- in which HACKER is careful to check everything he does. As described so far, HACKER is a pattern-directed problem-solving interpreter like PLANNER [Note 9]. This is fine as long as everything is working correctly, but what happens when either

1. There is no program in the Answer Library matching the problem statement?
   or
2. The program fetched fails to operate correctly in the prevailing problem environment?

HACKER is a computer programmer! If he doesn't have code available to solve a problem he writes some, and if any of his programs fail to operate correctly, he debugs them.

Proposal of programs

If there is no Procedure in the Answer Library which matches the problem posed, a program must be proposed to solve the problem. There are two ways by which a new program can be created by HACKER's program proposer.

1. By generalization of a piece of code previously written to solve a different but "similar" problem
   or
2. By application of a more general plan whose pattern of applicability matches the problem statement.

First HACKER's Notebook is examined to determine if he has ever before written code to satisfy a similar goal. If it is possible to variabilize such a program, and the goal for which it was written, so that it matches the new problem, the old code is extracted and subroutinized (inserted in the Answer Library with its generalized pattern) so that it is deemed applicable in the new situation as well as the old one.

If no such code is found, HACKER examines his Programming Techniques Library and his Blocks World Knowledge Library (collectively, his "Bag of Tricks") for a pattern-directed displacement macro to expand and replace the problem statement. There are macros which change the representations of problems. For example, it is sometimes necessary to expand a definition. There are macros which expand problems of a particular form into code. Such a macro represents a possible imperative semantics for problems it will match -- this often results in a "canned loop". Finally, there are "tricks" about the details of the Blocks World. For example, a good way to get rid of a block is to put it on the table. Usually there are several possible ways of writing a program to solve a particular problem. The program proposer attempts to select the most specific plan available (as measured by a fairly gross syntactic criterion). If that eventually fails (it may be undebuggable or unrefinable) more general methods are tried until one is found to be usable. Thus, the program proposer contains an implicit combinatorial search. In the discussion I will only show the ultimately successful paths. All code written by HACKER is extensively commented in HACKER's Notebook for debugging and future subroutinization.

Bugs

The proposed program is then passed to a criticizer, which checks to see if the program proposer has fallen into any of the known traps. If a potential bug is found, a patch is concocted to prevent it. The patch is commented in HACKER's Notebook and the program is recriticized. If no potential bugs are found, the new code is then passed to the interpreter for running (all new code is run CAREFULly).

Suppose a piece of code is run and a bug becomes manifest (it was overlooked by the criticizer). A call is made to the error system, which analyzes the situation in light of general knowledge about the types of bugs that can occur. The bug is classified. In some cases, where excess caution was applied and we have a false alarm, the program is continued at the point of interruption. In other cases, it is a known type of bug for which a patch can be made, and sometimes abstracted (summarized as a critic) so that it will not be overlooked at criticism time in the future. If the bug cannot be classified it is called an Anomalous Situation for which HACKER proceeds in a special mode.

Underlying this whole mechanism is a classical (PLANNER-like) pattern-directed problem solver. What we are looking at, the HACKER-Structure, is the mechanism by which the search is directed, and by which the results of search, both success and failure, are, where possible, generalized and summarized for future use. HACKER-Structure is the mechanism by which skill is acquired.

The HACKER Structure

This organization, the HACKER Structure, has an important virtue: The knowledge of the Blocks World is not spread uniformly throughout the system. In the initial (unskilled) state of HACKER, specific Blocks World information is contained only in some primitives in the Answer Library and in some definitions and facts contained in the Blocks World Knowledge Library. As HACKER practices (and becomes more skilled) the Answer Library, HACKER's Notebook, and the Critics' Gallery come to contain a deeply intertwined mess of Blocks World Knowledge and Programming Knowledge. The initial programming knowledge -- contained in the Programming Techniques Library, Types of Bugs, Types of Critics, Types of Patches, and in the structure of HACKER -- is generally applicable to any problem domain (though it is hardly complete even for so simple a world as the Blocks World). Thus HACKER possesses a very strong kind of generality: The problem domain is independent of the problem-solving mechanism. HACKER can therefore be applied to other domains without modification, though the Programming Techniques Library, Types of Bugs, Types of Critics, and Types of Patches would certainly have to be extended. Extension of HACKER may not be all that easy. Though the initial Blocks World knowledge is maintained in a very modular form, the programming knowledge is not at all modular. Any addition to or change in the Programming Techniques Library will require classification of the appropriate Types of Bugs, Types of Critics, and Types of Patches.

IV. Learning About CLEARTOP

In problem 1.1 HACKER examines his Answer Library for a subroutine whose pattern of applicability matches the problem statement:

(MAKE (ON A B))

He finds a subroutine which matches:

(TO (MAKE (ON a b))
    (PUTON a b))

This subroutine is just a call to the primitive block-moving subroutine PUTON, which puts the object a (the value of variable a) on the surface b (the top of any flat object is a surface), provided that there is nothing on a and there is a place for a on b. Thus when this answer is run it successfully solves problem 1.1.
This subroutine we dredged out of the Answer Library must be understandable by HACKER, for debugging. Thus HACKER must be able to comment it, and its parts. Special structures are provided to supply the program and its parts with names for use in comments. In this case we see that the program is given the name MAKE-ON and the first (and only) step is named M01:

(TO (MAKE (ON a b))
    (HPROG MAKE-ON
        (LINE M01 (PUTON a b))))

For the sake of clarity I will often leave out these syntactic details when they are irrelevant to the discussion.
HACKER's Notebook contains some initial comments about this program:

(GOAL MAKE-ON (MAKE (ON a b)))

27

(PURPOSE MO1 (MAKE (ON a b)) MAKE-ON)

These are not very exciting, but such comments can be very important.

In problem 1.2 this simple program cannot work because A is on B, so B cannot be moved by PUTON (only one object can be moved by a primitive!). The problem, (MAKE (ON B C)), however, matches the applicability pattern of MAKE-ON, so it is tried. The bug is manifest in PUTON, who complains:

(BUG UNSATISFIED-PREREQUISITE (NOT (ON A B)))

It is saying: "I cannot do my job because A is on B." This calls the debugging mechanism, specifically a program for UNSATISFIED-PREREQUISITE type bugs, which attempts to classify the bugs into subclasses which determine the kind of action to be taken. The subclassification is based solely upon the structure of the process in which the bug occurred, and not on any properties of the problem domain. Details of bug classification, and what I mean by the structure of the process, are made clear in Chapter IX, Types of Bugs. The bug classifier decides that this is a bug of the form PREREQUISITE-MISSING (an UNSATISFIED-PREREQUISITE might, for example, be caused by the prerequisite being clobbered). Just what is the generalized prerequisite which is missing, and how should it be patched? Looking up the stack, HACKER finds the line, MOI, that the bug appeared in. The code for that line is (PUTON a b). He then does a pattern-directed search of the database looking for prerequisites of (PUTON a b). One such statement is explicitly in the Blocks World Knowledge Library:

(FACT (PREREQUISITE (PUTON x y) (PLACE-FOR x y)))

Is this the guilty party? A subproblem is generated (which requires code to be written to answer it; we will ignore this detail):

(TEST (PLACE-FOR a b))

This test returns TRUE, there is a place on b=C for a=B. So this cannot be the problem. Looking more deeply, HACKER finds:

(FACT (PREREQUISITE exp (CLEARTOP obj))
      (HAVE () (MOVES exp obj)))

which says: "An expression has the prerequisite (CLEARTOP obj) if its execution will move that object." But HACKER knows that the primitive PUTON moves things:

(FACT (MOVES (PUTON x y) x))

Hence, another subproblem is generated to see if this is the culprit:

(TEST (CLEARTOP a))

But (CLEARTOP a) where a=B is false, so this must be the bug-causing prerequisite. (If none can be found, something strange is happening; see Chapter XIV, Anomalous Situations.) The bug is finally classified:

(PREREQUISITE-MISSING MAKE-ON MO1 (CLEARTOP a))

How is the bug to be fixed? The bug description (above) from the classifier is sent to the patch generator who looks up a patch:

(FACT (PATCH (PREREQUISITE-MISSING prog line prereq)
            (NEWLINE prog
              (ACHIEVE prereq)
              (((ACHIEVE prereq) line)))))

which says, "To fix this kind of bug, insert a new line in the buggy program to achieve the prerequisite." The inserter then inserts (see Chapter XII, Details of Program Construction) a line to (ACHIEVE (CLEARTOP a)) for MO1 in the program MAKE-ON. The program now reads:

(TO (MAKE (ON a b))
    (HPROG MAKE-ON
      (LINE L1   (ACHIEVE (CLEARTOP a)))
      (LINE MO1 (PUTON a b))))

HACKER's Notebook now also contains the "comment":

(PURPOSE L1 (ACHIEVE (CLEARTOP a)) MO1)

HACKER then restores the state of the world to the beginning of MAKE-ON, and restarts the program there.

Note: Like MAKE, ACHIEVE has no *a priori* meaning to HACKER. (ACHIEVE exp) is used so as to mean: "If exp is untrue, MAKE it true".

Line L1 is run, but there is nothing in the Answer Library to match (ACHIEVE (CLEARTOP a)). Thus a call is made to the program proposer for help. The program proposer looks around for a fact matching:

(CODE (ACHIEVE (CLEARTOP a)) code)

It finds nothing quite so specific, but in the Programming Techniques Library it comes up with:

(FACT (CODE (fun pat) code)
    (HAVE (mean) (MEANING-OF pat mean)
        (CSETQ code !"(fun mean))))

Sorry about the fancy syntax; I have no better way to write it. Anyway, this means that if you are trying to write code for a function (in this case ACHIEVE) of a pattern (in this case (CLEARTOP a)), and if the pattern has a meaning, then you can substitute the meaning for the pattern. Now, in the Blocks World Knowledge Library there is:

(FACT (MEANING-OF (CLEARTOP x)
        (NOT (EXISTS (y) (ON y x)))))

i.e. cleartop[x] <==> ~∃y on[y,x]

Thus the problem has been transformed from (ACHIEVE (CLEARTOP a)) to (ACHIEVE (NOT (EXISTS (y) (ON y a)))). Doesn't look too good, does it? But, in the Programming Techniques Library, a nice fact is found:

(FACT (CODE (ACHIEVE (NOT (EXISTS vars pat)))
        (UNTIL vars (CANNOT (ASSIGN vars pat))
            (MAKE (NOT pat)))))

Thus the problem (ACHIEVE (CLEARTOP a)) has become:

(UNTIL (y) (CANNOT (ASSIGN (y) (ON y a)))
    (MAKE (NOT (ON y a))))

A program! UNTIL is a canned loop which binds the variables which are the first argument. Then it runs its second argument and terminates if truth is returned, else it runs the third argument and repeats. Hence these instructions say: "Remove objects from the top of a until there are no more." As each of these transformations is performed, the old code is displaced by the results of the transformation, so now the subroutine reads:

```
(TO (MAKE (ON a b))
 (HPROG MAKE-ON
    (LINE L1 (UNTIL (y) (CANNOT (ASSIGN (y) (ON y a)))
                        (MAKE (NOT (ON y a)))))
    (LINE M01 (PUTON a b))))
```

HACKER reruns the modified Ll. UNTIL evaluates the predicate (CANNOT (ASSIGN ...)). One of the primitive abilities in the Blocks World is to be able to find an object on a given one; in fact, the Answer Library contains a primitive (we won't show you the body):

```
(TO (ASSIGN (u) (ON u v)) ... )
```

Since A is on B and a=B, y is assigned to A and the predicate fails. The program proceeds to (MAKE (NOT (ON A B))). The Answer Library is devoid of anything for this, but we find in the Programming Techniques Library:

```
(FACT (CODE (fun pat) code)
        (HAVE (suf) (SUFFICES-FOR pat suf)
            (CSETQ code !"(fun suf))))
```

Just like the fact about meanings, this says that we can substitute a sufficient condition for a pattern. Now in the Blocks World Knowledge Library we just happen to have:

```
(FACT (SUFFICES-FOR (NOT (ON x y))
        (EXISTS (z) (NOT (= z y)) (ON x z))))
```

i.e.: $\sim$on[x,y] $\Longleftarrow$ $\exists z{\neq}y$ on[x,z]

That is, for x not to be on y it suffices that there be a z≠y which x is on. Note that here EXISTS has three arguments: the list of bound variables, the qualifier, and the quantified expression. This is the standard form of a restricted existential quantifier, as used by mathematicians. I have chosen to use this rather than the logicians' "equivalent", in which the qualifier and quantified expression are conjoined, because this form is more expressive, as we shall see. The previous instance of EXISTS, in the definition of CLEARTOP, used the unrestricted quantifier. This is treated by HACKER as an abbreviation for the restricted case in which the qualifier is empty.

So (MAKE (NOT (ON y a))) is displaced with (MAKE (EXISTS (z) (NOT (= z a)) (ON y z))). In order to make this true, we must pick out a z≠a for which it is possible to satisfy (ON y z), and then use that z to make (ON y z) true. In the Programming Techniques Library it says just that:

```
(FACT (CODE (MAKE (EXISTS vars qual scope))
            (CHOOSE vars sels
                (AND (TEST qual)
                     (TEST (POSSIBLE scope)))
                (MAKE scope)))
       (CSETQ sels (SELECTOR vars)))
```

Hence, (MAKE (EXISTS (z) (NOT (= z a)) (ON y z))) is displaced with:

```
(CHOOSE (z) ((SURFACE z))
    (AND (TEST (NOT (= z a)))
         (TEST (POSSIBLE (ON y z))))
    (MAKE (ON y z)))
```

This program binds the variable z and selects a value for it from the set of SURFACEs. It tests that z≠a and that (ON y z) is possible. If z passes the test, the (MAKE (ON y z)) is executed and the CHOOSE returns. If z doesn't pass, the next surface is tried. It should be a mystery to you how HACKER knows that z is to be selected from the set of SURFACEs, rather than, say, OBJECTs. This mystery is resolved in Chapter XV, Formal Objects. Let's just assume here that it works by magic.

The new expression is run and z is assigned to a SURFACE. (A SURFACE is either the TABLE or any OBJECT with a flat top.) The surface is now tested. By some elementary facts:

```
(FACT (CODE (TEST (NOT (= x y))) (NOT (= x y))))
```

```
(FACT (CODE (TEST (POSSIBLE exp))
            (NOT (PROTECTED? (NOT exp))))))
```

the test is simplified. The first SURFACE chosen is always TABLE. TABLE≠a and we have no reason to avoid putting y on TABLE. (For an explanation of PROTECTED? see Chapter XIII, Protection Mechanism.) So control passes to (MAKE (ON y z)) with z=TABLE. But this is a call to the MAKE-ON just patched. Hence y=A is put on TABLE, then there are no more y's on B so B is put on C and the program returns to command level, solving problem 1.2. After problem 1.2 the program in the Answer Library is:

```
(TO (MAKE (ON a b))
  (HPROG MAKE-ON
    (LINE L1 (UNTIL (y) (CANNOT (ASSIGN (y) (ON y a))))
             (CHOOSE (z) ((SURFACE z))
                (AND (NOT (= z a))
                     (NOT (PROTECTED? (NOT (ON y z))))))
             (MAKE (ON y z)))))
    (LINE M01 (PUTON a b))))
```

I have neglected to tell you about the comments that get attached to each expression constructed by macro expansion and displacement, indicating how it was constructed. These will be used in subroutinization. (See Chapter X, Generalization and Subroutinization. A description of these commments may be found in Chapter XII, Details of Program Construction.)

I have also neglected to show you, as you have been warned, the failure paths which were explored in the construction of the code for CLEARTOP. You have only seen the successful result of the search process. It is important to notice that this result has been generalized, summarized, and remembered as a patch in an important routine in the Answer Library. Thus the search for how to (ACHIEVE (CLEARTOP a)) need never be done again. Indeed, as we will see in Chapter VI, this result will become more valuable when it is further generalized to become a subroutine in its own right. This summarization process is an essential part of skill acquisition.

This program, MAKE-ON, as modified in problem 1.2, is just tested in 1.3 on an isomorphic problem. In 1.4 we see its generality. Rather than just patching in for one case, HACKER has really understood the problem with the original MAKE-ON as demonstrated by its failure in 1.2.

Philosophical note

Before continuing, I want to make a point of the generality and extensibility of the methods demonstrated in this section. It is important to see how independent HACKER is of the problem domain. Clearly the Programming Techniques Library contains facts totally independent of the problem domain, and to change problem domain we need only supply a different Blocks World Knowledge Library. The debugging of the unsatisfied prerequisite is also done in a perfectly self-contained way. We might say that HACKER really knows how to solve problems in two distinct subject areas -- the Blocks World and Computer Programming -- and he uses techniques from both in this example. I like to say that HACKER is an example-driven problem solver who operates out of a "bag of tricks", special macros which offer, for each kind of problem encountered, a chunk of program appropriate to that kind of problem. A kind of trick which is not in HACKER's Programming Techniques Library but which would be necessary for, say, a HACKER whose domain is numerical analysis, would be the concept of successive approximation, as in square root. We all know the form of program:

```
     <pick a first approximation>
LOOP(COND (<is the approximation good enough?>
           (RETURN <the approximation>)))
     (SETQ approximation (better approximation))
     (GO LOOP)
```

To make an expert computer programmer out of HACKER one would have to formalize this into a FACT in the Programming Techniques Library, along with all of the others I have ignored. How many are there anyway? Is it 50, 500, 5000? I do not know, but I bet it's closer to 50 than 5000. I have formalized several kinds of bugs in HACKER as well. I haven't put in such obvious ones as "fencepost", but I could. How many bugs does an expert programmer know? We'll have to wait and see.

V. Learning About ON-chains

In problem 2.1, (MAKE (AND (ON A B) (ON B C))), there is no subroutine in the Answer Library which matches the problem. The program proposer is then called for help. The program proposer looks for a way to write the required code. There is a Programming Techniques Library method for AND of any number of subgoals. The implications of this technique are very complex and represent a major section of HACKER's theory of programming because most bugs arise from the unexpected interaction of simultaneous subgoals. However, in the absence of experience with the particular subgoals being considered, the AND technique makes the "linear" assumption that the subgoals are independent and thus can be sequentially achieved in an arbitrary order (it chooses the order of the problem statement). Now, in general, as we see in 2.1, this is not true, but it is a good working assumption provided that we realize that it is an assumption and are prepared to catch and fix the bugs that result when the assumption proves false. Thus the initial piece of code which HACKER writes looks like:

```
(HPROG AND2
       (LINE L3 (ACHIEVE (ON A B)))
       (LINE L4 (ACHIEVE (ON B C))))
```

HACKER also supplies comments:

```
(GOAL AND2 (MAKE (AND (ON A B) (ON B C))))
(PURPOSE L3 (ACHIEVE (ON A B)) AND2)
(PURPOSE L4 (ACHIEVE (ON B C)) AND2)
```

This means that, for example, the purpose of line L3 (the source) is to (ACHIEVE (ON A B)) for AND2 (the target). Line L3 attempts to run, but there is no Answer Library program for (ACHIEVE (ON A B)), only for (MAKE (ON A B)). But the Programming Techniques Library tells HACKER:

```
(FACT (CODE (ACHIEVE goal)
            (UNLESS (TEST goal) (MAKE goal)))))
```

So L3 gets clobbered by macro-expansion to:

```
(HPROG AND2
    (LINE L3 (UNLESS (TEST (ON A B))
                     (MAKE (ON A B))))
    (LINE L4 (ACHIEVE (ON B C))))
```

UNLESS is a conditional which executes its second argument if its first argument is false. It is a primitive ability of the Blocks World to be able to test if one block is on another, so the Answer Library contains a subroutine:

```
(TO (TEST (ON x y)) ...  )
```

This subroutine returns FALSE, so we proceed to (MAKE (ON A B)) using the routine generated in Scenario Section 1. Next we try to run line L4. Again, we do not have an answer in the Answer Library which matches (ACHIEVE (ON B C)), so the program proposer is called. The program proposer notices (see Chapter X, Generalization and Subroutinization, for an explanation of how) that it has written code for just such a goal (in line L3), and there is no reason to believe that that code cannot be generalized. The piece of code is extracted, subroutinized, and placed in the Answer Library:

```
(TO (ACHIEVE (ON u v))
    (HPROG E5
        (LINE L6 (UNLESS (TEST (ON u v))
                         (MAKE (ON u v)))))))
```

The point in AND2 where the code was created is replaced by a subroutine call:

```
(HPROG AND2
    (LINE L3 (ACHIEVE (ON A B)))
    (LINE L4 (ACHIEVE (ON B C))))
```

Looks like we're back where we started, but now we have a new subroutine in the Answer Library. Line L4 tries to run again. B is not on C so we (MAKE (ON B C)). This calls MAKE-ON (from Chapter IV, Learning About CLEARTOP). Line L1 in MAKE-ON finds that A is on B, and that will never do; so a place on TABLE is chosen for A and a recursion is made to (MAKE (ON A TABLE)). Line L1 finds that A has nothing on it and so line MO1 runs to (PUTON A TABLE). If things were just what they seemed to be, the program would now just put A on the TABLE, and then, satisfied that B had a clear top, would place B on C, and return, grinning. But HACKER, since he has just written AND2, and since he knows that new code cannot be trusted, watches the execution very closely (by interpreting the code in CAREFUL mode). In this mode the comments associated with each line of code are also interpreted, in a special way: For each line interpreted, on entry, those PURPOSE comments having the current line as the target are de-activated. The line is then run. Afterwards, each comment whose source is the current line is activated. During the time a comment is active, the purpose is protected so that if some side effect occurs which destroys the purpose of that comment, an interrupt to the error system is initiated (see Chapter XIII, The Protection Mechanism). The target of a purpose may, as in this case, be a program name. The scope of such a purpose terminates when the program returns. Thus in this case we have:

(PURPOSE L3 (ACHIEVE (ON A B)) AND2)
(PURPOSE L4 (ACHIEVE (ON B C)) AND2)

We see that the purpose comment of L3 was active during the execution of L4. Thus, during the execution of (PUTON A TABLE) to (CLEARTOP B) for (PUTON B C) for L4, an interrupt occurred to the error system, complaining:

(BUG PROTECTION-VIOLATION <L3>)

This error comment goes to the bug classifier, which looks at the structure of the process. The classifier decides, by techniques independent of the problem domain (see Chapter IX, Types of Bugs), that this bug is of the form PREREQUISITE-CLOBBERS-BROTHER-GOAL; that is, in program AND2 the subgoal of line L3, (ACHIEVE (ON A B)), was clobbered by the prerequisite, (CLEARTOP B), of the brother subgoal (ACHIEVE (ON B C)). This is formalized:

```
(PREREQUISITE-CLOBBERS-BROTHER-GOAL AND2 L3 L4
        (CLEARTOP B))
```

This is sent off to the patch-generator, who finds in his bag of tricks:

```
(FACT (PATCH (PREREQUISITE-CLOBBERS-BROTHER-GOAL
            prog line1 line2 prereq)
        (BEFORE line2 line1)))
```

an instruction to change the ordering of L3 and L4 in AND2.

Let us return to the original trick for AND expressions. We see that it produces a program consisting of a series of lines. A program is inherently ordered and there are often constraints on this ordering. For example, it is necessary that if the purpose of one line is to do something for some other line then the former must precede the latter. These constraints leave arbitrary some choices; they usually do not yield a unique program. Every program written or patched by HACKER is at that time sorted according to the ordering constraints (see Chapter XII, Details of Program Construction). In Chapter IV, where the prerequisite (ACHIEVE (CLEARTOP a)) was inserted in MAKE-ON, line L1 found its place before MO1 because of its purpose:

```
(PURPOSE L1 (ACHIEVE (CLEARTOP a)) MO1)
```

Back to AND2. The patcher has decided to reorder L3 and L4 in AND2 by adding a constraint forcing L4 to precede L3. AND2 is then re-sorted with this criterion, yielding:

```
(HPROG AND2
        (LINE L4 (ACHIEVE (ON B C)))
        (LINE L3 (ACHIEVE (ON A B))))
```

This program is then backed up to the beginning (restoring the configuration of blocks at its start) and re-executed. It works.

AND2 has been fixed, but it would be nice to be able to abstract the essence of the bug and patch which were so carefully worked out here and make use of it at the level of program construction so that we do not make the same mistake again. A general mechanism for this purpose, called criticism, has been provided in the program proposer. Before a program is released for use, it is held up to criticism. The program proposer effectively reads the program aloud (by adding the PURPOSE comments on each line to the data-base, in the order the lines appear). This airing is observed by critics (who are IF-ADDED methods [Note 10]), who leave nasty messages for the program proposer if they determine that there is a bug. (See Chapter XII, Details of Program Construction.) At the end of the reading the program proposer looks in his mailbox and finds the complaints. They may instruct him to insert lines, or re-sort them if another ordering rule is found. The program proposer executes the criticisms and then re-airs the program. This process terminates when either the mailbox is empty or an impossibility is discovered (such as two lines, each of which has to be before the other).

In this case, a critic is compiled (see Chapter XI, Critic Compilation) to formalize the lesson of AND2:

```
(WATCH-FOR
       (ORDER (PURPOSE 1line (ACHIEVE (ON a b)) t)
              (PURPOSE 2line (ACHIEVE (ON b c)) t))
       (PREREQUISITE-CLOBBERS-BROTHER-GOAL
          current-prog 1line 2line (CLEARTOP b)))
```

The variabilization of A, B, and C is done by the same mechanism as is used for subroutinization. This statement, which is further compiled into an IF-ADDED method, says that if, in the order specified, you see two purpose comments matching the ones shown, then leave a message to patch for the given kind of bug.

It is important to note here that criticism, like patching and subroutinization, is a way of summarizing and remembering knowledge gained by experience. Subroutines and patches retain, in a useful form, knowledge of positive results, how to do things correctly. Critics, however, retain important negative results. They remember the bad results of mistakes, so that they can be recognized in the future.

It should not be surprising that the caveat generated by solving problem 2.1 solves 2.2 as well. It is a general statement of the fact that structures are to be built bottom-up. Since this fact is now available to the program sorter, no error of ordering of this kind will ever again occur.

VI. Learning About Space Allocation

This chapter is about "space", a very general and exceedingly difficult concept. Spatial ideas are not just used in the descriptions of the motions and relations of physical objects. Space is an effective metaphor in most other aspects of symbolic human thought. The computer programmer thinks of "space" in memory and speaks of "high core", "the top of the stack", "under the loader". Not only is he using spatial terms like high, top, and under to describe relationships between entities in this abstract space, he also thinks of the entities themselves as physical objects which one can stack up or as enclosures to be loaded. Even in budgetary matters we see spatial metaphors: "Another ten-thousand dollars would give me 'room' to maneuver." Mathematicians have named abstract structure classifications, for example, "vector space", "topological space", and "function space" to emphasize their historical relationship to an intuitive spatial model. Even more striking, however, is the mathematician's extensive recourse to the diagram as a heuristic aid. Even those working in so abstract a subject as category theory "picture" their thoughts with arrows on the worksheet.

This generality of the notion of space is a mixed blessing. Anything we can say about space is generally applicable to a variety of problem-solving situations, but it is generally very difficult to say anything about space. Though space is a primitive notion in the description of many phenomena, we have a rather poor vocabulary for precisely describing spatial relations. The generality of the spatial concepts we can describe gives them great power. "Two things cannot occupy the same place at the same time" applies equally to data in registers and to blocks in a scene. The difficulty of description of spatial concepts makes them difficult to manipulate. Though CLEARTOP has an explicit meaning and we can formulate a sufficient condition for NOT-ONness, no such simple constructs work for PLACE-FOR. Here we must rely upon various strategies, no one of which is guaranteed to work, nor is the failure of one an indication of ultimate failure. Each strategy is expected to bring us "closer" to the goal (PLACE-FOR a b). Thus, whole new structures must be introduced to enable the effective use of each strategy in each instance and to coordinate them when such is called for.

Space is a "stuff" that comes in quantities, or "chunks". A chunk may be either "free" or "used" but not both. If used, a chunk has one or more "users" who "occupy" subchunks. A chunk can be returned to the free state by "moving" each of its users to a disjoint chunk. Implicit in the notions "stuff" and "chunk" are conservation of quantity (the total amount of space is a constant) and a notion of contiguity (that chunks are contiguous blocks of space). Space also has directions.

In problem 3.1 HACKER examines his Answer Library for a subroutine whose pattern of applicability matches the problem statement: (MAKE (ON C B)). The matching subroutine, last patched in Scenario Section 1 is:

```
(TO (MAKE (ON a b))
     (HPROG MAKE-ON
          (LINE L1 ... )
          (LINE MO1 (PUTON a b)))))
```

This program worked fine in 3.1 because there was enough space on B for C, satisfying the requirements of PUTON.

In problem 3.2, however, this program is tried and fails to work because no place is found for C on B, as A is smack in the middle of B. PUTON complains:

```
(BUG UNSATISFIED-PREREQUISITE (PLACE-FOR C B))
```

As in Scenario Section 1, this bug is patched by prerequisite insertion in the program MAKE-ON. The patch is, as before, introduced as follows:

```
(TO (MAKE (ON a b))
     (HPROG MAKE-ON
          (LINE L1 ...)
          (LINE L5 (ACHIEVE (PLACE-FOR a b)))
          (LINE MO1 (PUTON a b)) ))
```

where:

```
(PURPOSE L1 (ACHIEVE (CLEARTOP a)) MO1)
(PURPOSE L5 (ACHIEVE (PLACE-FOR a b)) MO1)
(PURPOSE MO1 (MAKE (ON a b)) MAKE-ON)
(GOAL MAKE-ON (MAKE (ON a b)))
```

Line L5 is run, but there is no answer in the Answer Library matching (ACHIEVE (PLACE-FOR a b)). The program proposer is called, who finds a Programming Technique, introduced earlier:

```
(FACT (CODE (ACHIEVE goal)
            (UNLESS (TEST goal) (MAKE goal))))
```

which transforms the problem into:

```
(UNLESS (TEST (PLACE-FOR a b))
        (MAKE (PLACE-FOR a b)) )
```

HACKER knows how to test (PLACE-FOR a b) (even the primitive PUTON can do it!) as there is an answer:

```
(TO (TEST (PLACE-FOR x y)) ... )
```

The test is run (a=C, b=B) and returns FALSE. Thus the interpreter continues, executing (MAKE (PLACE-FOR a b)). There is again no answer in the Answer Library matching this, so the program proposer is called. PLACE-FOR has no explicit meaning or sufficient condition; nor does it have a nice (known) form like (NOT (EXISTS ...)). The program proposer does find, however, a Programming Technique:

```
(FACT (CODE (MAKE goal) code)
   (HAVE (culprit) (MAY-HURT goal culprit)
      (COND ((TEST1 culprit)
             (CSETQ code (TRYOUT goal culprit))))))
```

This says, "Do I know of any condition (the culprit) the truth of which might inhibit the truth of the goal pattern? If so, and if the culprit is currently true, write code which tries to improve things." (TRYOUT is a function which writes the code; we shall see the result.) Just such a condition is found in the Blocks World Knowledge Library:

(FACT (MAY-HURT (PLACE-FOR x y) (NOT (COMPACT y))))

Is (NOT (COMPACT b)) a possible culprit? A subproblem,
(TEST (NOT (COMPACT b))) where b=B, is generated (and some
code is written for it; we ignore this detail). The answer is yes, as:

(FACT (MEANING-OF (COMPACT x)
         (FORALL (y) (ON y x) (LEFTMOST y))))

That is, every object on x has no space on its left. But A is on B
and has space on its left. Thus this is a possible reason why
(PLACE-FOR C B) is false, so TRYOUT writes the following code
which displaces (MAKE (PLACE-FOR a b)):

(STRATEGIES-FOR (TEST (PLACE-FOR a b))
    (HPROG S6
        (LINE L7 (TRY (COMPACT b)))))

with comments:

(GOAL S6 (MAKE (PLACE-FOR a b)))
(PURPOSE L7 (TRY (COMPACT b)) S6)

STRATEGIES-FOR is a control primitive designed for running
strategies for solving a problem. It binds one internal variable to its
first argument, the success condition, and another to its control
frame [Note 11]. It then evaluates its second argument, the strategies
themselves. As we shall see, a strategy will use this information to
periodically test whether it has succeeded, and if so, to exit from the
STRATEGIES-FOR. If control ever returns to the STRATEGIES-
FOR from the evaluation of its second argument, the strategies tried
have failed, and HACKER is called for help.
    Next, line L7 is run. By meaning substitution, we get:

(STRATEGIES-FOR (TEST (PLACE-FOR a b))
    (HPROG S6
        (LINE L7 (TRY (FORALL (z) (ON z b) (LEFTMOST z))))))

How is the COMPACT strategy to be implemented? We could
(ACHIEVE (COMPACT b)) using:

```
(FACT (CODE (ACHIEVE (FORALL vars qual scope))
       (UNTIL vars
           (CANNOT (ASSIGN vars
                          (AND qual (NOT scope))))
           (MAKE scope))))
```

to get:

```
(UNTIL (z)
   (CANNOT (ASSIGN (z)
                  (AND (ON z b) (NOT (LEFTMOST z)))))
   (MAKE (LEFTMOST z)))
```

However, it would be foolish to completely compact the top of an object with many objects on it; we might only have to move one block to make space. Thus, every time we move a block (increasing the compactness), we should check if there is now a PLACE-FOR a on b. This Programming Technique is a slight perturbation of the above:

```
(FACT (CODE (TRY (FORALL vars qual scope))
       (UNTIL vars
           (CANNOT (ASSIGN vars
                          (AND qual (NOT scope))))
           (MAKE scope)
           (DONE?))))
```

which expands our stuff into:

```
(STRATEGIES-FOR (TEST (PLACE-FOR a b))
  (HPROG S6
    (LINE L7 (UNTIL (z)
                (CANNOT (ASSIGN (z)
                               (AND (ON z b)
                                   (NOT (LEFTMOST z)))))
                (MAKE (LEFTMOST z))
                (DONE?)))))
```

Here DONE? is a function which executes the first argument of STRATEGIES-FOR (as accessed via the internal variable bound to it). If the test succeeds, the strategy has succeeded and DONE? performs an exit from STRATEGIES-FOR.

This new program begins to run. It tries to (ASSIGN (z) (AND (ON z b) (NOT (LEFTMOST z))))) This has no known answer, but an ASSIGN can always be turned into a CHOOSE via a complex fact (FACT (CODE (ASSIGN vars exp) (CHOOSE ...))) which is very hairy but not worth explaining. This expansion results in (for readability we will suppress line and program labels unless they are relevant):

```
(STRATEGIES-FOR (TEST (PLACE-FOR a b))
  (UNTIL (z) (CANNOT (CHOOSE (u) ((OBJECT u))
                              (TEST (AND (ON u b)
                                         (NOT (LEFTMOST u))))
                              (CSETQ z u)))
             (MAKE (LEFTMOST z))
             (DONE?)))
```

The same magic (explained in Chapter XV, Formal Objects) was used here as in Chapter IV to realize that u is to be selected from the class of OBJECTs. The

```
(TEST (AND (ON u b) (NOT (LEFTMOST u))))
```

is run (on the first object selected) and expanded into:

```
(AND (TEST (ON u b)) (NOT (TEST (LEFTMOST u))))
```

via

```
(FACT (CODE (TEST (NOT exp)) (NOT (TEST exp))))
```

and

```
(FACT (CODE (TEST (AND exp1 exp2))
            (AND (TEST exp1) (TEST exp2))))
```

(actually this is generalized to any number of expressions using fancy pattern matching syntax).

The Blocks World has the primitive perceptual ability to (TEST (ON u b)) and (TEST (LEFTMOST u)). Hence since b=B, the only u on b is A, which is not as left as possible, hence z is set to A. The next step interpreted is (MAKE (LEFTMOST z)). This further reduces to (PUSH z LEFT) via a Blocks World Knowledge Library fact:

```
(FACT (CODE (MAKE (LEFTMOST a)) (PUSH a LEFT)))
```

Thus the final code looks like:

```
(STRATEGIES-FOR (TEST (PLACE-FOR a b))
     (UNTIL (z) (CANNOT (CHOOSE (u) ((OBJECT u))
                            (AND (ON u b)
                                 (NOT (LEFTMOST u)))
                         (CSETQ z u)))
              (PUSH z LEFT)
              (DONE?))))
```

This code pushes A to the left, making room for C on B. It then returns control to STRATEGIES-FOR, which returns to L5, which proceeds to MO1, which puts C on B as required by problem 3.2.

    Now let's go on to problem 3.3. In this case the top of B is completely filled with A and C, and the problem is (MAKE (ON D B)). MAKE-ON is called with a=D and b=B. D has a clear top so we go to L5. There is no place for D on B so the test fails and we enter the strategies and thus COMPACT. In this case, however, there is no block on B which has space to its left, so the COMPACT strategy fails. STRATEGIES-FOR has no more strategies so it calls HACKER for help. HACKER keeps a list of the strategies already used in building S6. He looks in the data-base to see if there are any around which haven't been incorporated. Of course, one is found:

```
(FACT (MAY-HURT (PLACE-FOR x y) (CLUTTERED y)))
```

where

```
(FACT (MEANING-OF (CLUTTERED a)
          (EXISTS (z)
               (POSSIBLE (NOT (ON z a)))
               (ON z a))))
```

This strategy is inserted:

```
(HPROG S6
    (LINE L7 ... )
    (LINE L8 (TRY (NOT (CLUTTERED b)))))
```

with comment:

```
(PURPOSE L8 (TRY (NOT (CLUTTERED b))) S6)
```

L8 is now run, and expanded into:

```
(LINE L8
  (UNTIL (z) (CANNOT (ASSIGN (z)
                        (AND (POSSIBLE (NOT (ON z b)))
                             (ON z b))))
          (MAKE (NOT (ON z b)))
          (DONE?)))
```

using the Programming Technique:

```
(FACT (CODE (TRY (NOT (EXISTS vars qual scope)))
            (UNTIL vars (CANNOT (ASSIGN vars
                                    (AND qual scope)))
                   (MAKE (NOT scope))
                   (DONE?))))
```

The (ASSIGN (z) ...) is run, expanding, as before, into a CHOOSE expression:

```
(CHOOSE (u) ((OBJECT u))
    (TEST (AND (POSSIBLE (NOT (ON u b))) (ON u b)))
    (CSETQ z u))
```

the test expression of which expands into:

```
(AND (NOT (PROTECTED? (ON u b))) (TEST (ON u b)))
```

Now both objects A and C are on B and the position of neither is protected. Thus, if C is selected first (as in problem 3.3) z gets assigned C. Control then passes to the business end:

```
(MAKE (NOT (ON z b)))
```

Now, something interesting happens! Did you notice it? HACKER once before had to remove an object from another; in the expansion of (ACHIEVE (CLEARTOP a)) it was necessary to write code for (MAKE (NOT (ON y a))). HACKER notices this, and by magic (see Chapter X, Generalization and Subroutinization) extracts the code written before, subroutinizes it, and adds it to the Answer Library, so it can be used here (and elsewhere, if needed):

```
(TO (MAKE (NOT (ON y a)))
  (HPROG E9
    (LINE L10
      (CHOOSE (z) ((SURFACE z))
        (AND (NOT (= z a))
             (NOT (PROTECTED? (NOT (ON y z))))))
        (MAKE (ON y z))))))
```

So now, E9 is called and, as a result, C is placed on the table. Control then passes to the (DONE?) which succeeds and so D is placed (by MO1) where C was on B. Thus, HACKER has solved problem 3.3.

At this point we should look at MAKE-ON for some perspective, leaving out LINEs and HPROGs:

```
(TO (MAKE (ON a b))
  (UNTIL (y) (CANNOT (ASSIGN (y) (ON y a)))
            (MAKE (NOT (ON y a))))
  (UNLESS (TEST (PLACE-FOR a b))
    (STRATEGIES-FOR (TEST (PLACE-FOR a b))
      (UNTIL (z)
        (CANNOT (CHOOSE (u) ((OBJECT u))
                   (AND (ON u b) (NOT (LEFTMOST u)))
                   (CSETQ z u)))
        (PUSH z LEFT)
        (DONE?))
      (UNTIL (z)
        (CANNOT (CHOOSE (u) ((OBJECT u))
                   (AND (NOT (PROTECTED? (ON u b)))
                        (ON u b))
                   (CSETQ z u)))
        (MAKE (NOT (ON z b)))
        (DONE?))))
  (PUTON a b))
```

Remember how this rather complex program started out (at the beginning of Chapter IV)? It still isn't finished; as we shall see, there are some bugs to attend to, but the worst is over. I really haven't been honest about the comments; there are expansion comments (HPROGs and LINEs) all over this program (for truth, see Chapter XII, Details of Program Construction) but they have been systematically suppressed everywhere except the most interesting places, to improve readability.

As for problem 3.4, we see that this program works immediately. The COMPACT strategy is immediately rejected so we go on to the CLUTTERED strategy. In choosing an object to remove from B, only D passes the test because (ON A B) is protected, so D is removed, making room for C, which is then placed in the newly cleared space.

Problem 3.5 is, however, an interesting twist on the kind of debugging demonstrated in Chapter V. The comments on lines L7 and L8 are:

(PURPOSE L7 (TRY (COMPACT b)) S6)
(PURPOSE L8 (TRY (NOT (CLUTTERED b))) S6)

In trying to get D on B in problem 3.5, we find that there is no place for D. Compacting is tried. This results in C being pushed left to abut A. No more compacting can be done because all objects on B are in their LEFTMOST position. Next we try uncluttering B. The only removable object is A because (ON C B) is protected. Thus A is selected for removal. In attempting to put A on the TABLE, however, a protection violation happens because removing A makes B no longer COMPACT, as C suddenly has space on its left, and we are still in the scope of the purpose of line L7. An analysis of this situation suggests, but does not guarantee, that L7 and L8 should be interchanged. (See Chapter IX, Types of Bugs, for details of the method of debugging.) The situation is described as:

(STRATEGY-CLOBBERS-BROTHER S6 L7 L8)

Since there is no known reason why they shouldn't be interchanged, they are interchanged, and a new critic is entered for future reference:

```
(WATCH-FOR
  (ORDER (PURPOSE line1 (TRY (COMPACT b)) t)
         (PURPOSE line2 (TRY (NOT (CLUTTERED b))) t))
  (STRATEGY-CLOBBERS-BROTHER
         current-prog line1 line2))
```

The program is now backed up to the beginning of S6; C is back where it started. The new program then removes A first, generating enough space for D, which is then placed correctly, completing the task required.

Scenario problem 3.6 just once again demonstrates prerequisite insertion and subroutinization. It is necessary to (PUSH C LEFT) to compact the space on B so A can be placed. However, as in PUTON, PUSH will not move more than one object at a time. Since D is on C, PUSH complains:

```
(BUG UNSATISFIED-PREREQUISITE (NOT (ON D C)))
```

Now the debugger decides, as in Chapter IV, that this is a bug of type PREREQUISITE-MISSING. Since:

```
(FACT (MOVES (PUSH obj dir) obj))
```

(CLEARTOP z) is the culprit as in Chapter IV. Where do we insert (ACHIEVE (CLEARTOP z))? I have nicely avoided showing the expansion comments around (PUSH z LEFT) in L7. They were created when the expression (MAKE (LEFTMOST z)) was expanded to (PUSH z LEFT). We need them now, so use your big magnifier to see that what I wrote as (PUSH z LEFT) really is:

```
(HPROG E30
       (LINE L31 (PUSH z LEFT)))
```

The prerequisite is now inserted:

```
(HPROG E30
       (LINE L32 (ACHIEVE (CLEARTOP z)))
       (LINE L31 (PUSH z LEFT)))
```

with comments:

```
(GOAL E30 (MAKE (LEFTMOST z)))
```

```
(PURPOSE L31 (MAKE (LEFTMOST z)) E30)
(PURPOSE L32 (ACHIEVE (CLEARTOP z)) L31)
```

Time is backed up to the beginning of E30 and then the program is continued. The interpreter encounters (ACHIEVE (CLEARTOP z)) but HACKER remembers writing code for that in L1. The code is extracted and placed in the Answer Library:

```
(TO (ACHIEVE (CLEARTOP a))
  (HPROG E33
    (LINE L34 (UNTIL (y) (CANNOT (ASSIGN (y) (ON y a)))
                    (MAKE (NOT (ON y a)))))))
```

L1 is patched to call the new routine:

```
(LINE L1 (ACHIEVE (CLEARTOP a)))
```

Now D is removed from C and put on the TABLE, C is moved to the left, and A is placed as required.

We leave Scenario Section 3 with a well-developed mechanism for making space if none is available, and two new routines in the Answer Library: (TO (MAKE (NOT (ON a b))) ...) and (TO (ACHIEVE (CLEARTOP a)) ...). It is appropriate to take a final look at MAKE-ON in its mature form with all HPROGs and LINEs suppressed:

```
(TO (MAKE (ON a b))
  (ACHIEVE (CLEARTOP a))
  (UNLESS (TEST (PLACE-FOR a b))
    (STRATEGIES-FOR (TEST (PLACE-FOR a b))
        (UNTIL (z)
            (CANNOT (CHOOSE (u) ((OBJECT u))
                            (AND (NOT (PROTECTED? (ON u b)))
                                 (ON u b))
                            (CSETQ z u)))
            (MAKE (NOT (ON z b)))
            (DONE?))
        (UNTIL (z)
            (CANNOT (CHOOSE (u) ((OBJECT u))
                            (AND (ON u b) (NOT (LEFTMOST u)))
                            (CSETQ z u)))
            (ACHIEVE (CLEARTOP z))
            (PUSH z LEFT)
            (DONE?))))
  (PUTON a b))
```

VII. Learning About Space Conflicts

At first glance, Scenario Section 4 appears to deal with a (perhaps minor) inefficiency. In the mind of an experienced programmer, however, apparent inefficiency is not a minor consideration; it may be an indication of a fundamental difficulty. While it may seem on the surface that an intelligent person is wasting hours over a few microseconds, he may in fact be doing an agonizing algorithmic analysis which will result in a qualitatively "better" program.

For example, suppose problem 4.1 was (MAKE (AND (ON A C) (ON D A) (ON B C))) rather than simply (MAKE (AND (ON A C) (ON B C))). In this case, A would be placed on the middle of C, D on A, and then, to put B on C it would be necessary to push A, which has D on it. Hence D must be removed, resulting in a PROTECTION-VIOLATION. Thus what looked like a minor matter of efficiency has turned out to be a bug!

In order that HACKER be aware of this kind of situation, those Blocks World primitives which actually move objects (PUTON and PUSH) check, when executed in CAREFUL mode, whether the object which is about to be moved has ever been moved before. (As described in Chapter IX, Types of Bugs, HACKER retains the entire history of the problem-solving process until it returns to command level. This information is used to answer the question.) If it is discovered that an object, say A, is being moved for the second time, a call is made to the error system to check the possibility of trouble:

(BUG DOUBLE-MOVE A)

Usually, as we shall see in the next chapter, no trouble is developing and the error system just dismisses the interrupt as a false alarm, allowing the program to proceed.

In problem 4.1, however, the command is (MAKE (AND (ON A C) (ON B C))). As usual in cases of no special knowledge, HACKER makes the "linear" assumption that the goals do not interact and that they can be achieved linearly and independently:

```
(HPROG AND11
     (LINE L12 (ACHIEVE (ON A C)))
     (LINE L13 (ACHIEVE (ON B C))) )
```

with the standard comments:

```
(GOAL AND11 (MAKE (AND (ON A C) (ON B C))))
(PURPOSE L12 (ACHIEVE (ON A C)) AND11)
(PURPOSE L13 (ACHIEVE (ON B C)) AND11)
```

L12 is run and A is placed in the middle of C (using the subroutine (TO (ACHIEVE (ON u v)) ...) developed previously). A is moved and a note is made of this. Next, line L13 is run. B is not on C, so a call is made to (MAKE (ON B C)). B has a clear top but there is no (PLACE-FOR B C) because A is in the way. The strategies developed (in the previous chapter) are tried. Since (ON A C) is protected by L12, nothing can be removed from the top of C. The next strategy tried, compaction, discovers that A is not in a LEFTMOST position on C and thus tries to (PUSH A LEFT). At this point it is noticed that A is being moved for the second time in this problem, resulting in the error call: (BUG DOUBLE-MOVE A).
        Observing that brother lines L12 and L13 are fighting over the prerequisite calculations:

```
(ACHIEVE (PLACE-FOR A C))
(ACHIEVE (PLACE-FOR B C))
```

the error system (see Chapter IX, Types of Bugs) classifies the situation:

```
(PREREQUISITE-CONFLICT-BROTHERS AND11
     ((PLACE-FOR A C) L12)
     ((PLACE-FOR B C) L13))
```

This is sent to the patch-generator for a fix. The patch-generator looks for a patch which matches; he finds:

```
(FACT (PATCH (PREREQUISITE-CONFLICT-BROTHERS prog
                 (pre1 line1)
                 (pre2 line2))
          (NEWLINE prog
              (RESOLVE (ACHIEVE pre1) (ACHIEVE pre2))
              (((ACHIEVE pre1) line1)
               ((ACHIEVE pre2) line2) ))))
```

Actually, this fact is written for any number of line-prerequisite pairs but it is shown here for only two in the interest of clarity. Thus the patch will be effected by executing:

```
(NEWLINE AND11
      (RESOLVE (ACHIEVE (PLACE-FOR A C))
               (ACHIEVE (PLACE-FOR B C)))
      (((ACHIEVE (PLACE-FOR A C)) L12)
       ((ACHIEVE (PLACE-FOR B C)) L13)))
```

But this will insert a new line in AND11:

```
(HPROG AND11
      (LINE L14 (RESOLVE (ACHIEVE (PLACE-FOR A C))
                         (ACHIEVE (PLACE-FOR B C))))
      (LINE L12 (ACHIEVE (ON A C)))
      (LINE L13 (ACHIEVE (ON B C))) )
```

with comments:

```
(PURPOSE L14 (ACHIEVE (PLACE-FOR A C)) L12)
(PURPOSE L14 (ACHIEVE (PLACE-FOR B C)) L13)
```

Before looking at what L14 expands into, and thus how the new AND11 works, it is necessary to understand more about HACKER's notions of space, specifically the deeper structure and interaction of the primitives PUTON and (TO (TEST (PLACE-FOR a b))...). In order to understand how to control the placing of A on C so that room is left for B, we must examine how a place is chosen for A on C. With a really big magnifier, we can look inside the "primitive" PUTON (though HACKER never does). We find, essentially (but simplified):

```
(CDEFUN PUTON (obj surface)
    (MUST (OBJECT obj) (SURFACE surface))
    (UNLESS (FIRST-MOVE obj)
            (BUG DOUBLE-MOVE obj))
    (UNLESS (CANNOT (ASSIGN (z) (ON z obj)))
            (BUG UNSATISFIED-PREREQUISITE
                          (NOT (ON z obj))))
    (UNLESS (TEST (PLACE-FOR obj surface))
            (BUG UNSATISFIED-PREREQUISITE
                          (PLACE-FOR obj surface)))
    (MOVE obj (GHOST obj surface)))
```

First it declares the types of its arguments (this is used in Chapter XV, Formal Objects). Next it checks if the object has been moved before. Then it makes sure that there is nothing on the object about to be moved. Finally it checks that there is space available. If all the checks are OK, it moves the object to the coordinates specified by (GHOST obj surface). What is the GHOST and how did it appear? To answer this question, we note that PUTON called (TEST (PLACE-FOR obj surface)). This test is truly perceptual magic, details of which are discussed in [Note 12], the FINDSPACE Problem. In any case, this test first checks if either obj or a GHOST of obj is already on the surface. If so, it is immediately satisfied. If not, it searches (by number-crunching the analytic geometry descriptions of the objects) for an open space on surface big enough to hold obj. If it finds one, obj is "imagined" centered there. This is represented by the erection of a GHOST of obj in that place on surface. A GHOST is <u>not</u> the object it represents. A GHOST can be imagined to be somewhere even if the object it represents cannot be moved because stuff is piled on it. A GHOST is a purely perceptual entity. It "occupies" the space of the object it represents, and thus is a kind of reservation for space to be filled later. No object can be moved into the chunk of space occupied by the GHOST of another object. Any perceptual calculations dealing with space, such as another (TEST (PLACE-FOR obj1 surface)) must contend with the GHOST, which is as real for these calculations as an object. A GHOST is not, however, an object. It cannot be referred to in non-primitive code; nor can it be moved. A GHOST generated during the execution of a program disappears when either the object it represents is moved to fill it or the system returns to command level.
       The first argument of (TEST (PLACE-FOR arg1 arg2)) is

not limited to atomic objects. If a list of objects is passed, for example:

(TEST (PLACE-FOR (A B) C))

the test determines if there is simultaneously room available for A and B on top of C, and if so, erects GHOSTs for both A and B. Thus if (PUTON A C) and (PUTON B C) are later executed, A will fill its GHOST and B will fill its GHOST. Since both GHOSTs were on C, the places which A and B will occupy are guaranteed disjoint. Hence, this is the solution to our problem, how to expand L14:

(RESOLVE (ACHIEVE (PLACE-FOR A C))
         (ACHIEVE (PLACE-FOR B C)))

We return to AND11 which is now backed up and rerun. The Blocks World Knowledge Library must know all this stuff about GHOSTs, in fact:

(FACT (CODE (RESOLVE (ACHIEVE (PLACE-FOR x z))
                     (ACHIEVE (PLACE-FOR y z)))
            (ACHIEVE (PLACE-FOR (x y) z))))

Actually, this fact is stated here for only a two-way fight to give you an idea of how it works. HACKER really knows this in the general case. Thus the final code is:

(HPROG AND11
       (LINE L14 (ACHIEVE (PLACE-FOR (A B) C)))
       (LINE L12 (ACHIEVE (ON A C)))
       (LINE L13 (ACHIEVE (ON B C))))

Now, how is this patch knowledge generalized to make problem 4.2 work immediately?

L14 is like nothing we have ever encountered previously in this document. It is a prerequisite for two lines, neither of which would need help if standing alone. Such lines are often found in programs written by people. In fact, programs abound with lines which are neither directly related to achieving the goal of the program (unlike L12 and L13, which are main steps), nor prerequisite to any other specific step, but rather are present to prevent destructive interference between other steps. We call these variously setups (like L14), interfaces (if they go between steps), and cleanups (if they go after the steps in question). For example, consider the problem of computing the values of both x/3 and x+4, where x is the contents of accumulator X, in PDP-10 assembly language. Each subcalculation can be achieved in one instruction (IDIVI X,3 and ADDI X,4). Either instruction, however, destroys x, so a copy must be made before either is executed:

```
MOVE A,X
IDIVI X,3
ADDI A,4
```

In this case, things are even hairier than in AND11 because the ADDI must fetch its argument from A rather than X to work correctly. HACKER must be able to handle such problems of interface. In this case, a new critic is compiled for the bug of type PREREQUISITE-CONFLICT-BROTHERS (see Chapter XI, Critic Compilation, for details of how), to oversee future program construction (see Chapter XII, Details of Program Construction, for how it is used). The new critic is:

```
(WATCH-FOR
  (GIVEN (c t) (MORE-THAN-ONE (a line)
                   (PURPOSE line (ACHIEVE (ON a c)) t)))
    (PREREQUISITE-CONFLICT-BROTHERS current-prog
        (EXPAND (line (PLACE-FOR a c)))))
```

This watches for any surface c and purpose target t for which more than one line is being compiled with the purpose of putting more than one object a on c for t. If such a case is found, the bug PREREQUISITE-CONFLICT-BROTHERS should be expected. The prerequisites in conflict are the (PLACE-FOR a c)'s for all the lines so noticed.

Thus, for problem 4.2, (MAKE (AND (ON A D) (ON B D) (ON C D))), the main steps are to achieve each subgoal. This program is held up for criticism and our new critic complains that there will be a bug unless a patch is made. Thus the program proposer does the patch before releasing the new program. The resulting code is:

```
(HPROG AND15
    (LINE L16 (RESOLVE (ACHIEVE (PLACE-FOR A D))
                       (ACHIEVE (PLACE-FOR B D))
                       (ACHIEVE (PLACE-FOR C D))))
    (LINE L17 (ACHIEVE (ON A D)))
    (LINE L18 (ACHIEVE (ON B D)))
    (LINE L19 (ACHIEVE (ON C D))) )
```

which works immediately, once L16 is expanded.

VIII. Showing Off

In this Section we watch HACKER do just one problem:

```
(MAKE (AND (ON D A) (ON B E) (ON A E)
           (ON C E) (ON F D))),
```

Here the skills developed in the previous training sequence are displayed. Since there is no answer in the Answer Library for this conjunction, the problem goes off to the program proposer, who first proposes (to himself) the linear theory program:

```
(HPROG AND20
       (LINE L21 (ACHIEVE (ON D A)))
       (LINE L22 (ACHIEVE (ON B E)))
       (LINE L23 (ACHIEVE (ON A E)))
       (LINE L24 (ACHIEVE (ON C E)))
       (LINE L25 (ACHIEVE (ON F D))) )
```

The comments on this code are now read to the critics. Besides the built-in critic who insures that prerequisites go before the lines they serve, we now have two new critics who embody the knowledge that: "Before anything is placed on an object, that object must be placed" and "If more than one object is to be placed on one surface, space must be reserved for each of the objects on the surface before any is placed." These critics could be named the "Tower Critic" and the "Floorplan Critic".

L21 is read off, but nothing much happens. The reading of L22 is similarly uninteresting. L23, however, fires off both critics. The Tower Critic notices that A is being moved (to put it on E) after D was put on A. This is an order error which requires that L23 be brought before L21. The Floorplan Critic notes that since both B and A are being placed on E, some preliminary planning will be needed. Next, L24 is read off, causing the Floorplan Critic to amend his advice to include C on E along with B and A. When line L25 is read off nothing bad is noted. The program proposer now reads his mail and implements the changes requested, that L23 be placed before L21 and that a special space-planning line be inserted before L22, L23, and L24. The resulting program looks like:

```
(HPROG AND20
    (LINE L26  (RESOLVE (ACHIEVE (PLACE-FOR B E))
                        (ACHIEVE (PLACE-FOR A E))
                        (ACHIEVE (PLACE-FOR C E)) ))
    (LINE L23 (ACHIEVE (ON A E)))
    (LINE L21 (ACHIEVE (ON D A)))
    (LINE L22 (ACHIEVE (ON B E)))
    (LINE L24 (ACHIEVE (ON C E)))
    (LINE L25 (ACHIEVE (ON F D))) )
```

The program is now re-aired. Since no more criticisms accrue, it is released for use. Line L26 is run and expanded into:

```
(LINE L26 (ACHIEVE (PLACE-FOR (B A C) E)))
```

There is no space for anything on E because F is on E. The two-strategy program written and debugged in Chapter VI is called. The first strategy is tried: Is there any object on E which can be removed? F is on E without good reason, so it is removed and placed on the table. The test is now run, and now there is room on E for the composite object (B A C). Hence the test succeeds, after erecting ghosts on E for B, A, and C. Line L26 returns to AND20 and next L23 is run. A is to be placed in its ghost (on the middle of E). But D is on A so when Ll (the CLEARTOP line written in Chapter IV) is run, D is placed on the table, then A is moved to fill its place on E. Next, line L21 is run, and D is moved for a second time -- an interrupt occurs which examines the situation and determines that it is OK, not one of the known bug types; the interrupt is dismissed -- and placed on A. L22 is run, B is to be placed on E, but first B must have a CLEARTOP so C is removed and put on the table. Then B is put on E. L24 is run and C is placed on E. Here again, an interrupt on DOUBLE-MOVE is made and dismissed. (In a more intelligent system than HACKER this would not be so easily dismissed. C didn't have to be moved twice because it could have been placed correctly the first time. Fixing this would require a complete reorganization of the CLEARTOP program so that it could take non-local advice from a free variable whose value would be set by AND20 initially. Perhaps this is an indication of where one could attack the "overview" problem.) Finally L25 is run, F is balanced on D. F has also been moved twice, but no error is noted and the program proceeds as expected, completing the solution.

IX. Types of Bugs

In this chapter we will examine the processing of bugs. We will follow this processing from the point at which a bug is detected through the time at which a patch is determined.

Entry to the error system

There are three ways by which a bug may become known to the error system:

1. A primitive may be called to perform a task impossible for that primitive. For example, PUTON may be told to move an object which cannot be moved (as a primitive operation) because there is an object supported by the object to be moved. The primitive makes its complaint directly to the error system, passing it the error comment UNSATISFIED-PREREQUISITE and what it would need to be true (in this instance) for the commanded action to be possible. In conventional programming, most error comments are of this type. If, for example, one tries to divide by zero or take the square root of a negative number, any reasonable programming system will complain and not allow the program to continue. (Clever systems allow the user to specify what to do in such a situation, if he wants to extend the meanings of the primitives.)

2. The error system may also be called from the protection monitor (see Chapter XIII, The Protection Mechanism) if a protected subgoal is clobbered between the time it is established and the time it is no longer needed. This results in an interrupt of the performance program, a call to the error system with the error comment PROTECTION-VIOLATION and a specification (to be explained) of the protection violated. This kind of error comment does not really occur in conventional programming, though good programmers often insert consistency checks into their programs to test for "impossible" situations.

3. Finally, the error system may be called if the performance program violates some "aesthetic" principle of the particular knowledge domain being manipulated. For example, in the Blocks World it is unaesthetic to move an object twice in the same problem. This may not be a real bug, but it is worth investigating because it may point at an important interaction. In the Blocks World primitives there are explicit checks for double move problems, which result in calls to the error system with the error comment DOUBLE-MOVE and a descriptor of the first move. Again, in human programming there is no counterpart to an aesthetic interrupt unless, for example, the programmer notices that his program is doing something stupid, like calculating the same result twice.

In any case, when a (potential) problem is noticed and passed off to the error system, we say that a bug has become manifest.

Before we go on to examine in detail what happens when a bug becomes manifest we should consider just what class of bugs can be caught by these kinds of "local" processing techniques. Is it possible, for example, for a program to have no UNSATISFIED-PREREQUISITE or PROTECTION-VIOLATION errors on a particular problem and still be incorrect in the sense that the program terminates with the overall goal unachieved? The protection mechanism prevents a program from continuing after clobbering a result which is needed later. Thus, the only way a program can terminate with its goal unachieved is for some part of the goal never to be achieved. This can happen in only two ways: either there is no step in the program, one of whose purposes is to achieve the missing part of the goal; or the step in the program whose purpose is to achieve the missing part of the goal is not working correctly. In the latter case we are back where we started from -- we have a step terminating without achieving its purpose. Thus, if there are no infinite loops or recursions, the only way we can have a program failure get by without a protection scope violation is for the program to have a faulty plan -- one which makes no attempt to achieve some part of the goal.

In general, HACKER's debugging system can only handle almost-right programs -- programs which require only a slight perturbation such as rearrangement of steps, or insertion of auxiliary steps to provide for prerequisites or interface with other steps. This is consistent with the overall philosophy of evolutionary programming -- a program is always almost right, it just needs a small patch to make it work in the new situation. This of course puts a heavy burden on the program proposer to propose good first approximations. The burden is not fatal, however, because a bad plan will usually fail badly in the situation for which it is proposed, causing the proposer to backtrack and choose a new (and hopefully better) plan.

It is interesting to note that because of the comprehensive error detection system, HACKER has a far easier task than the human programmer. For the human there is often a problem in isolating the manifestation of a bug; a good deal of debugging time is spent "catching" and identifying the manifestation. Primitives often, for the sake of efficiency, do not check their prerequisites. In MACLISP [Note 13], for example, CAR when applied to an atom does not complain. It returns a useless undefined quantity which can be passed around without difficulty. Only later, when some other primitive tries to operate on the result, does the system stop and complain. By this time, of course, an indefinite computation has happened and it may be difficult to find out where the original problem occurred. The protection mechanism, under CAREFUL evaluation, also provides the ability to localize some bugs before they propagate. I have often spent long hours trying to find out how a variable whose value I am depending upon has been clobbered. It would be nice, when writing the code, to be able to specify (as a comment) those lines which depend upon a value being preserved, and then to be warned if the value is clobbered in the scope of such a protection.

Bug classification

When an error enters the error system we say that a bug is manifest; it is not yet, however, understood, in the sense that a patch can be rationally concocted to fix it. It is the function of the bug classifier to take a manifest bug and understand its underlying cause so as to instruct the patcher about a fix.

This step is necessary because, unfortunately, there is no one-to-one correspondence between bug manifestations and underlying causes. For example (and let us call this example NO-1-2.1 for later), suppose that in the Scenario, Section 1 never happened. Then in problem 2.1 the program MAKE-ON would not have line L1 in it to set up a (CLEARTOP a) for line MO1, (PUTON a b). If we pose problem 2.1, the program for (MAKE (AND (ON A B) (ON B C))) initially reads:

```
(HPROG AND2
    (LINE L3 (ACHIEVE (ON A B)))
    (LINE L4 (ACHIEVE (ON B C))))
```

When this program is run, L3 puts A on B and L4 tries to put B on C. But A is on B so PUTON complains:

```
(BUG UNSATISIFIED-PREREQUISITE (NOT (ON A B)))
```

However, in the real Scenario, with Section 1 before Section 2, the "same" bug became manifest as:

```
(BUG PROTECTION-VIOLATION <chrontext>)
```

where what I mean by the same bug is that the underlying cause of both instances is the same -- that a prerequisite of making (ON B C) true, (CLEARTOP B), is incompatible with the truth of (ON A B). Prerequisite insertion in this example is only a side issue, as such insertion will only convert the bug manifestation from an UNSATISFIED-PREREQUISITE to a PROTECTION-VIOLATION.

Now that we see why the bug classifier is needed, we should turn our attention to how it works. This is, however, a rather difficult problem, as the current bug classifier in HACKER is an *ad hoc* program, and thus the body of knowledge (called Types of Bugs in the overview flowchart) on which it operates is difficult to separate out and display. This, of course, makes Types of Bugs also very difficult to extend. The hope is, however, that Types of Bugs is essentially independent of the problem domain and need only be expanded when new problem-solving methods (the Programming Techniques Library) are introduced. An important area for development of HACKER-like problem-solving methods would be the systematization of the knowledge in Types of Bugs in a more modular form.

The bug classifier was written by introspection. I carefully watched myself debug programs having bugs of the types we shall examine and attempted to abstract the mechanism from my behavior. Thus another difficulty with explaining the bug classifier is that we must be sure to separate the actions of the bug classifier from the arguments for those actions and the deductions on which they are based due to the author.

First let us make some general observations. What does a

human programmer do when he has his program stopped at the first place where something has manifestly gone wrong? First he says, "What the ?<*! is my program doing?" and then he starts thinking. I actually think that his comment is revealing -- he is thinking about what his program is doing -- its dynamic behavior. Assuming he has a debugging system available, he examines:

1. the (lexical) locus of failure, reading nearby comments in his listing;
2. the dynamic environment -- the stack and the dynamic registers (variables) in this section of code.

He thinks about why control got here and how it did. The why can usually be ascertained from the stack and the comments; it looks like a string of "A called B to accomplish C for reason D." The how is more difficult, as it has a chronological component. He tries to reconstruct previous states of the computer and apply this how-why analysis to them. (Usually this is very difficult because information is lost.) In short, he produces a (partial) abstract model of the process which his program produced. This model contains both a temporal (how) and a teleological (why) component. The model is used in conjunction with the manifestation to compute the underlying cause, hence the patch. Please note that in this document the words "how" and "why" are technical words. They are being given precise meanings. Words are chosen to take on technical meanings by virtue of the mnemonic value of their everyday meanings which are perceived to relate to the technical meanings assigned to them. Numerous other such words have been used without comment, such as "purpose" and "goal".

Here again, HACKER has a distinct advantage over the human programmer. When in CAREFUL mode, a HACKER program leaves a chronological trace behind it, using the CONNIVER context mechanism [Note 14]. For each side effect, a new context frame is pushed on this chronological trace, the CHRONTEXT, so that at any point, say when a bug becomes manifest, HACKER has available to him a sequence of worlds, each incrementally different from the next, representing in reverse chronological order the series of states the world has been through as a result of the execution of the program. HACKER also has available to him the current control stack, and for each of the frames of CHRONTEXT he has the control stack as it was at the time of creation of that frame. This ability derives from the

CONNIVER control structure in which both HACKER and the programs he writes are embedded. HACKER is also aided by the fact that his code is completely commented with active comments which define the teleological structure of the process. The currently active PURPOSE comments are accessible by the bug classifier. They describe what the program is trying to accomplish. Let's see now how HACKER uses these structures which are available to him.

We have seen that there is no one-to-one correspondence between bug manifestations and underlying causes, so given a particular manifestation more information is needed to pick out a particular underlying cause. I claim that the bugs can be disambiguated by asking questions about the history and teleology of the process. For the bug types which I have classified there are six questions which perform this disambiguation. There are three possible manifestation types and six possible outcomes of which four are recognized underlying causes. Figure 2 gives an overview of bug classification. The questions and those paths through the classifier which occur in the Scenario will be discussed in the text following. Some of the questions are rather complex and cannot be reasonably presented without their explanation. For reference, however, the underlying causes are:

> PCB Prerequisite-Conflict-Brothers
> PM Prerequisite-Missing
> PCBG Prerequisite-Clobbers-Brother-Goal
> SCB Strategy-Clobbers-Brother

Going back to Scenario Section 1, when (PUTON B C) failed because A was on B, it complained to the error system by executing:

(BUG UNSATISFIED-PREREQUISITE (NOT (ON A B)))

The BUG function dispatched on the manifestation type, UNSATISFIED-PREREQUISITE, to some code prepared to handle that kind of manifestation. We note that PUTON sent an argument, (NOT (ON A B)), explaining specifically what it was upset about -- PUTON requires (NOT (ON A B)) to be true. Now, (ON A B) may be part of a currently protected subgoal. Thus the first question is:

1. Would it conflict with any of my current goals to make the

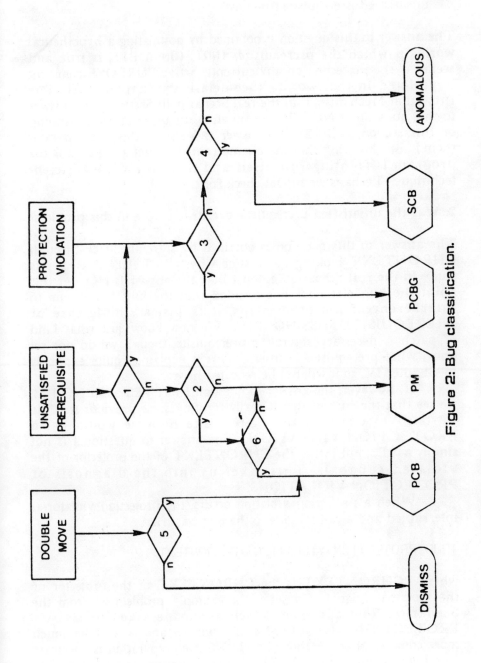

Figure 2: Bug classification.

unsatisfied prerequisite true now?

The answer to this question is obtained by postulating a hypothetical world in which the prerequisite, (NOT (ON A B)), is true and seeing if the protection on any currently active PURPOSE comment is violated in that world. (See details in Chapter XIII, The Protection Mechanism.) In the real Scenario, in Section 1, the answer to this question is NO. (In the situation discussed at the beginning of this section, NO-1-2.1, the answer is YES! so this test separates them.) But knowing that there is no conflict is not all; perhaps the program is fighting with itself and there is a more efficient technique. Perhaps we should check for this:

2. Was the unsatisfied prerequisite ever true before in this problem?

The answer to this question is obtained by searching back through CHRONTEXT looking for a time when (NOT (ON A B)) was true. In the real Scenario Section 1 bug, the answer is NO. At this point the bug classifier has decided that the bug is not due to interference from other steps, it is just a simple case of PREREQUISITE-MISSING (PM). We now know just what kind of patch is necessary, insert the prerequisite, though we do not yet know what prerequisite to insert. This is explained quite explicitly in Chapter IV, so it will not be repeated here.

If, however, the answer to question 1 was YES as in NO-1-2.1, we see that the current step is really fighting some previous step. If we tried to establish the prerequisite here we would get a PROTECTION-VIOLATION. The answer to question 1 is not simply a YES, but rather the CHRONTEXT of the protector of the violated subgoal. This takes us into the diagnosis of PROTECTION-VIOLATIONS.

When a protection violation occurs, the protection violator is interrupted and a call is made to the bug classifier:

(BUG PROTECTION-VIOLATION <PCHRONTEXT>)

where PCHRONTEXT is the CHRONTEXT of the protector of the violated subgoal. Consider, for example, problem 2.1 from the Scenario. The questions which are to be asked to classify PROTECTION-VIOLATIONs, questions 3 and 4, will be much more complex than questions 1 and 2. Some preparation is necessary (for both us and HACKER) before the questions can be answered (or even stated). Please examine Figure 3. You are looking at a model of the information available to the bug classifier at the time of failure in problem 2.1 due to the PROTECTION-VIOLATION. This is a chronological model; time increases to the right. It is not a linear representation with respect to time; I have expanded those sections of interest and shrunk those I am not interested in. Vertically, you are looking at the height of the control stack. Arrows pointing to the right are the scopes of PURPOSE comments; those which point into space are the purposes of main steps. There is one prerequisite arrow labeled (CLEARTOP B) pointing from the stack frame labeled L1:UNTIL to the one labeled MO1. Near the middle of the bottom line (the time base) is a small arrow marking the present (the bug manifestation point). Thus only stuff to the left of that arrow exists; the stuff to the right is deduced as follows:

We (the bug classifier) are given PCHRONTEXT and CHRONTEXT, the current state of the world. From CHRONTEXT, we can find the top of the stack, that frame marked MO1:PUTON. Somehow, it is violating the protection on the scope of the comment originating on L3 (from PCHRONTEXT). Why are we in MO1:PUTON? We can look up the purpose of MO1 in HACKER's NOTEBOOK:

(PURPOSE MO1 (MAKE (ON a b)) MAKE-ON)

Instantiating the current values of a and b (A and TABLE) we find that this is a main step of MAKE-ON. That, however, is a subcalculation of L1:UNTIL, which is a prerequisite calculation for an MO1 (yet to be called), which is a main step of MAKE-ON, which is a subcalculation of UNLESS, which is a subcalculation of L4:ACHIEVE-ON, which is a main step of the AND2. Thus, by looking at the stacks pointed at by PCHRONTEXT and CHRONTEXT, and the comments in the data-base about the code, we can construct an abstract teleological process model. This model is constructed and looks like Figure 4. In this figure, a box signifies a computation, an arrow a teleological link labeled by the subgoal. A teleological link points from the computation which makes the subgoal true to the computation which requires its truth. A plain arrow is a main-step link; a special arrow is used for prerequisites. Any number of consecutive main-step and subcalculation links form one main-step. The triangles labeled pc and c are the PCHRONTEXT and CHRONTEXT pointers respectively.

Now that we understand what a teleological process model

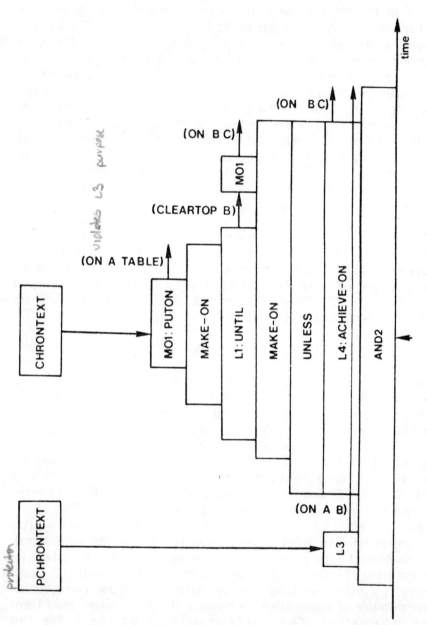

Figure 3: The process of problem 2.1.

looks like and how it is constructed from the information available at bug manifestation time, we can understand the meaning of question 3 and how it is to be answered.

3. Is the protection violator a prerequisite calculation (perhaps hypothetical) for a step whose purpose is to satisfy a brother goal (of a conjunction) to the one violated?

This question, about the structure of the teleological process model, is a pattern which is matched against the model (Figure 5). If the pattern matches, the bug is classified as of type PREREQUISITE-CLOBBERS-BROTHER-GOAL (PCBG). The PROTECTION-VIOLATION of problem 2.1 and the UNSATISFIED-PREREQUISITE of NO-1-2.1 are both of this type. For 2.1, the actual statement of classification is:

```
(PREREQUISITE-CLOBBERS-BROTHER-GOAL
    AND2 L3 L4 (CLEARTOP B))
```

Now that we have the underlying cause of the bug in problem 2.1, how can we patch it? The offending prerequisite must, in any case, be done before its step. Its scope must extend until that step. But since the first and second steps are brothers (they are both for the same target), their scopes must overlap. Thus, since the scope of the first step and the scope of the prerequisite of the second step are incompatible, the only way to prevent overlap is to move the second step before the first. This is summarized as:

```
(FACT (PATCH (PREREQUISITE-CLOBBERS-BROTHER-GOAL
                prog line1 line2 prereq)
             (BEFORE line2 line1))))
```

which when executed forces line2 to move up to before line1.

Just how much generality is there in the concept PCBG? Perhaps it is just peculiar to the Blocks World? In fact, PCBG is a very common form of non-linearity.

If, for example, one wants to paint the ceiling, it is simultaneously necessary that the paint be on the platform and that the painter be on the ladder. The linear strategy is to achieve each subgoal independently. The painter can either first lift the can to the ladder platform, and then climb the ladder, which works; or he can first climb the ladder and then lift the can, which doesn't work.

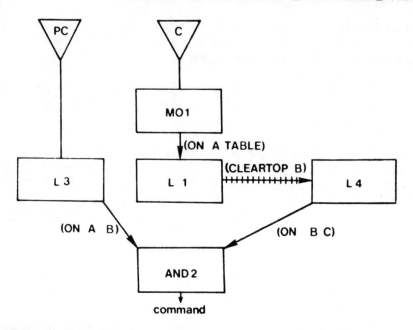

Figure 4: The abstract model of the PROTECTION-VIOLATION manifestation of problem 2.1.

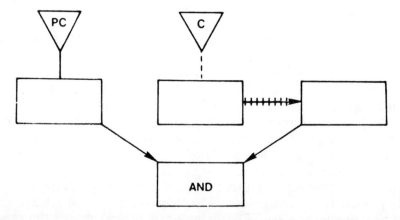

Figure 5: The pattern represented by question 3. The dotted line is any structure containing no prerequisite links.

Once he is on the ladder, he has no access to the can on the ground. He must first come down to get the paint (clobbering the previously achieved subgoal of being on the ladder). Climbing down -- to achieve the prerequisite to lifting the paint can -- has clobbered the brother goal of being on the ladder.

In programming, too, one often runs into PCBG's. Consider the problem of compiling the LISP expression (F 3 (G 4)). If the argument-passing convention is to load the arguments into successive argument registers and then call the function, we see that the call to function F requires that 3 be in register 1 and the result of (G 4) be in register 2. If we try the obvious order -- first put 3 in register 1, then calculate (G 4) and put it in register 2 -- we find that we must load 1 with 4 to call G, thus clobbering the brother goal of having 3 in register 1.

In Scenario problem 3.5 we encounter a different kind of protection violation. We won't go through the teleological model generation here, as it is just like before. The resulting abstract teleological process model for the bug manifestation occurring here is shown in Figure 6. There are several reasons why question 3 is false here. For one thing, there is no conjunction computation at all. In fact, here we are seeing a fight between two (hopefully) cumulative strategies for improving the chance that the desired goal, (PLACE-FOR D B), is true. In order to spot this kind of interaction so that it may be removed (if possible) to improve cooperation between the strategies, the bug classifier asks:

4. Is the protection violator a brother strategy to the one violated?

This question (see Figure 7) matches the situation in problem 3.5. The bug is recognized and classified by this pattern match as a STRATEGY-CLOBBERS-BROTHER (SCB). The underlying cause is:

(STRATEGY-CLOBBERS-BROTHER S6 L7 L8)

Now that we have classified this bug we must decide what to do to fix it. It is interesting to note that if we were in a conjunction, rather than a STRATEGIES-FOR, this would be a very touchy situation. The actual step causing the PROTECTION-VIOLATION is (PUTON A TABLE), a main step of the strategy (NOT (CLUTTERED B)), rather than a prerequisite step. In a conjunction both (COMPACT B) and (NOT (CLUTTERED B)) would

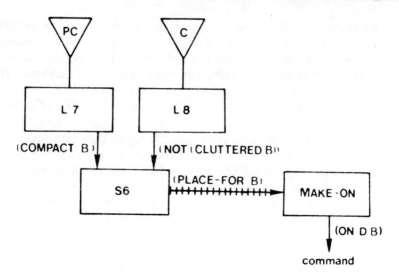

Figure 6: The abstract model of the PROTECTION-VIOLATION manifestation of problem 3.5.

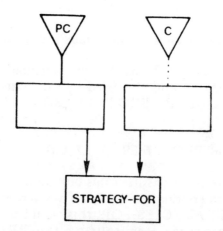

Figure 7: The pattern represented by question 4. Here the dotted line indicates any computation containing <u>not more than one</u> prerequisite link.

be expected to be true at the end (to satisfy the conjunctive goal). If (NOT (CLUTTERED B)) and (COMPACT B) were truly incompatible (contradictory) the required program would be impossible. Since we are in a STRATEGIES-FOR, however, there is no requirement for either (NOT (CLUTTERED B)) or (COMPACT B) to be true when STRATEGIES-FOR returns, only that (PLACE-FOR D B) be true. Hence even if we cannot resolve the conflict, this PROTECTION-VIOLATION is non-fatal. HACKER, however, hopes that the strategies are cumulative on the real goal, (PLACE-FOR D B). It is advantageous to reduce conflicts, if possible. It may help to interchange the strategies; thus the suggested patch:

```
(FACT (PATCH (STRATEGY-CLOBBERS-BROTHER
             prog line1 line2)
       (TRY-BEFORE line2 line1)))
```

TRY-BEFORE is not binding like BEFORE; if the resulting sort is over-determined, a TRY-BEFORE may be ignored. In this case the hope that the strategies are cumulative is realized.

   If a PROTECTION-VIOLATION bug occurs which cannot be recognized by either of the two previous patterns, it is deemed anomalous. An example of such a problem and how it is handled can be found in Chapter XIV, Anomalous Situations.

   In Chapter VII we meet another kind of bug call, (BUG DOUBLE-MOVE <PCHRONTEXT>), from the Blocks World aesthetics. It has much of the flavor of a protection violation. Whereas in a protection violation we are presented with an argument between the protector and the violator, here we are presented with a less serious argument between the first and second mover of an object, in this case A. I have only worked out the classification of one type of DOUBLE-MOVE situation characterized by a YES to question 5. We will see that question 5 is more complex than any of the preceding classifiers and must be broken into several steps.

   First, we look at the abstract teleological process model of the problem in question (see Figure 8). Because we are in a complex situation, a brief summary of the facts leading to this model is in order. At the present time (the bug is manifest) we are in (PUSH A LEFT), which is a main step for the (COMPACT C) strategy for (PLACE-FOR B C). (A strategy of a STRATEGY-FOR is a main step.) (PLACE-FOR B C), however, is the goal of L5, a prerequisite calculation for MO1:(PUTON B C). MO1 is a main step of MAKE-ON, which was called by UNLESS, which is a main step of ACHIEVE-ON, which was called by L13, a main step of AND11, a result of the command. The first move of A was in MO1:(PUTON A C), a main step of MAKE-ON, which was called by UNLESS, which is a main step of ACHIEVE-ON, which was called by L12, a brother step of L13 in AND11.

We see that Figure 8 is similar to Figure 4. The first component of question 5 reflects that similarity in its similarity to question 3:

5.1. Is the second mover a prerequisite calculation for a step whose purpose is to satisfy a brother goal (of a conjunction) to the first mover?

Question 5.1 is diagrammed in Figure 9. You will note that, in the pattern match, the prerequisite link is remembered in the variable pre. (Actually, in all the matches made, all boxes and lines are remembered for construction of the underlying cause specification. Here, however, the use is more conscious.) If 5.1 answers NO, question 5 fails. If 5.1 answers YES (as in problem 4.1, being discussed), we go on. The next subquestion is:

5.2. Was pre ever true before in this problem?

This subquestion is answered (as was question 2) by searching down CHRONTEXT for the first place where (PLACE–FOR B C) was true. In 4.1 it was certainly true at the beginning of the problem. It was not true after L12, (ACHIEVE (ON A C)). It was certainly not true after (PUTON A C). But it was not true even before the PUTON was executed. It became false when (TEST (PLACE–FOR A C)) was executed because that is when the GHOST of A was placed in the center of C. But that was done to (ACHIEVE (PLACE–FOR A C)), a prerequisite of (PUTON A C), the first mover of A. Let us call the CHRONTEXT where (PLACE–FOR B C) became false FCHRONTEXT, and extend our process model to include it (see Figure 10). The final step in the chain is:

5.3. Is FC a part of a prerequisite calculation for PC?

As we see in Figure 11, 5.3 is TRUE. This completes the chain of reasoning of question 5 successfully, resulting in the diagnosis of a

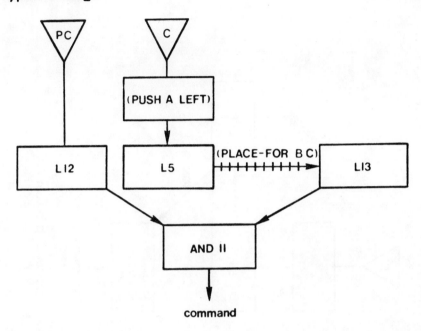

Figure 8: The abstract process model for the DOUBLE-MOVE manifestation in problem 4.1.

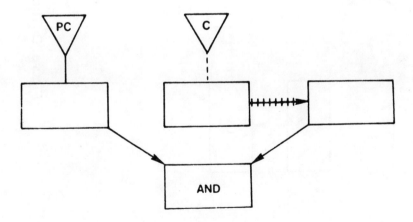

Figure 9: The pattern represented by question 5.1. The dotted line is any structure containing no prerequisite links.

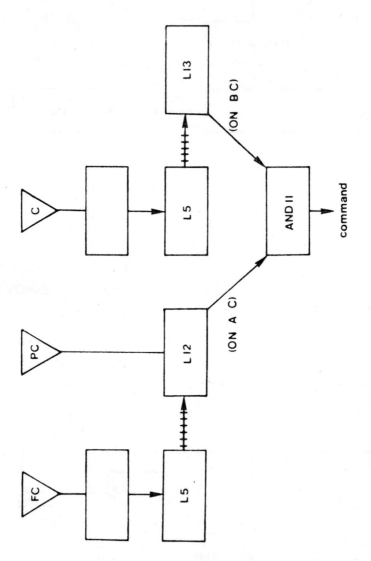

Figure 10: The extended process model of problem 4.1.

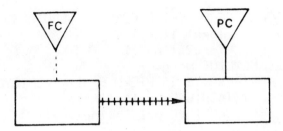

Figure 11: The pattern represented by question 5.3. The dotted line is any structure containing no prerequisite links.

PREREQUISITE-CONFLICT-BROTHERS (PCB):

```
(PREREQUISITE-CONFLICT-BROTHERS AND11
    ((PLACE-FOR A C) L12)
    ((PLACE-FOR B C) L13))
```

This diagnosis is certainly complex enough. Before we lose the forest for the trees, let's informally go through the diagnosis again. (ACHIEVE (PLACE-FOR A C)) is a prerequisite of (PUTON A C), a main step of one of a pair of brother subgoals. The other brother's main step, (PUTON B C), has (ACHIEVE (PLACE-FOR B C)) as its prerequisite. The (ACHIEVE (PLACE-FOR A C)) is choosing a place to put A. When (ACHIEVE (PLACE-FOR B C)) is called to find a place for B it finds itself moving A. Clearly there is a conflict. It would be nice to fix the conflict so that A wouldn't have to be moved twice. This would require that the chooser of a place for A know about the need for a place for B. But no one except AND11 knows that both A and B are going to be put on C. If anything can be done to fix this problem it must be done at the level of AND11 -- If two employees of an organization are fighting, the trouble is with their immediate joint superior: he must parcel out the tasks so that they do not conflict. That is just what the diagnosis said: "There is trouble in AND11, a conflict between L12 and L13. The trouble is that their prerequisites, as listed, conflict." Now, the bug patcher doesn't know how to resolve the conflict, as that is a detail of the problem domain. He does, however, know that such conflicts can be resolved by a special setup line before either L12 or L13, as described in Chapter VII:

```
(FACT (PATCH (PREREQUISITE-CONFLICT-BROTHERS prog
                (pre1 line1)
                (pre2 line2))
        (NEWLINE prog
            (RESOLVE (ACHIEVE pre1) (ACHIEVE pre2))
            (((ACHIEVE pre1) line1)
             ((ACHIEVE pre2) line2) ))))
```

It should also be clear that a PCB bug can be manifest as an UNSATISFIED-PREREQUISITE; that was what question 2 was about. I will not go into the precise description of question 6 which does this recognition. If you understood this chapter, you should have no trouble deriving it yourself.

To the Reader:

I hope you got through this section. I know that it is pretty tough, I had to write it! Debugging of computer programs is a difficult, intellectually challenging activity; we should expect it to be complex. I have only catalogued a few types of bugs, because it is so difficult. The important thing to see, however, is that debugging is at least to some extent independent of the problem domain; that some bugs are purely a result of the procedural representation (that things are done in sequential discrete steps); and that there is such a thing as a "programmer", an expert at procedural matters.

X. Generalization and Subroutinization

The central feature of HACKER is that he learns from experience, that he gets better with practice. In order that this be possible, HACKER must be able to apply the knowledge learned in the solution of a specific problem to the solution of new problems.

In some cases this is easy, as in the insertion and expansion of CLEARTOP in Scenario Section 1. The system knew (could deduce), from Blocks World Knowledge, that for any value of a in (PUTON a b) it is necessary that (CLEARTOP a) be true. Since this general prerequisite was inserted into, and expanded in, a program of general usefulness, MAKE-ON, the benefits of this discovery are automatically passed on. The essential improvement of performance comes from the fact that after this is learned, it becomes "second nature" to CLEARTOP an object before trying to put it on something. HACKER no longer has to worry about that particular complaint from PUTON, nor does he ever again have to perform the search (for how to CLEARTOP) summarized by the expansion. In Scenario Section 3, learning about space allocation, much the same is true; HACKER is again patching a generally useful program. Even the fix of the strategy misordering can proliferate to any program using MAKE-ON.

If there were no Answer Library, each problem would lead to the construction of a new program. Even though we could force future programs to be written correctly, using critics, all of the expansions would have to be done for each case, and an expansion can entail an exponential search. Thus, subroutines are an excellent means of maintaining a summary of valuable knowledge which has been deduced in creating and fixing them. It thus is appropriate for HACKER to attempt to subroutinize if possible, so that if a patch is made to a piece of code, the benefits are felt everywhere that code is called. This is not to say, however, that every intermediate step in an expansion should be subroutinized; this would only clog the Answer Library with large numbers of subroutines, most of which would never be called except from one routine. This would so break up the Answer Library that debugging would be more difficult --

the structure of the problem would not be reflected in the structure of the program. Hence, HACKER only subroutinizes when he notices that he is about to expand the "same" pattern for a second time. In this chapter I will explain how HACKER decides that two patterns are the "same". This is used not only in subroutinization, but also in compiling critics, as we shall see.

Consider the problem of determining just what it means for two problems, say (ACHIEVE (ON A B)) and (ACHIEVE (ON B C)), to be the "same". We COMBINE the two patterns, getting (ACHIEVE (ON {A B} {B C})) [Note 15]. The two problems are the same with respect to any manipulation (say the one which is the solution of the first problem) which does not depend upon the bracketed expressions being constant. Thus, a program written to solve (ACHIEVE (ON A B)) can be used for (ACHIEVE (ON B C)), with the appropriate substitution, if it was written without depending upon particular properties of the objects A and B. The problem, then, is to distinguish just what constants in the goal pattern (and the program) can be consistently variabilized. As we shall see in detail, HACKER solves this problem by monitoring what various expressions are matched against in the execution of the program under consideration for generalization. HACKER decides that a constant is unconstrained and hence may be variabilized only if it is never matched against itself in the execution of the program -- if it is always matched against variables only.

Exactly this problem comes up in the example in Scenario Section 2 where HACKER is trying to solve:

(MAKE (AND (ON A B) (ON B C)))

The AND trick proposes that this be solved by:

(HPROG AND2
      (LINE L3 (ACHIEVE (ON A B)))
      (LINE L4 (ACHIEVE (ON B C))))

where:

(GOAL AND2 (MAKE (AND (ON A B) (ON B C))))
(PURPOSE L3 (ACHIEVE (ON A B)) AND2)
(PURPOSE L4 (ACHIEVE (ON B C)) AND2)

One difficulty with AND2, besides the order error, is that at that point HACKER did not know how to (ACHIEVE (ON A B)), but only how to (MAKE (ON A B)). Thus in the running of L3 the fact

```
(FACT (CODE (ACHIEVE goal)
            (UNLESS (TEST goal) (MAKE goal)))))
```

was used to expand (ACHIEVE (ON A B)), getting

```
(HPROG AND2
    (LINE L3 (UNLESS (TEST (ON A B))
                     (MAKE (ON A B))))
    (LINE L4 (ACHIEVE (ON B C))))
```

Chapter V then goes on to explain that when running line L4 HACKER notices that the code written in L3 is good for L4 as well, and it gets extracted, generalized, and subroutinized. We are now about to understand how this is done.

At this point I'll have to admit that the code written for L3 is really slightly more hairy than I showed you. (You'll excuse my lying for clarity of exposition; the honest truth is explained at length in Chapter XII, Details of Program Construction.) The truth is:

```
(HPROG AND2
    (LINE L3
        (HPROG E5
            (LINE L6 (UNLESS (TEST (ON A B))
                             (MAKE (ON A B)))))))
    (LINE L4 (ACHIEVE (ON B C))))
```

Not much different, except for tags to add comments:

```
(PURPOSE L6 (ACHIEVE (ON A B)) E5)
(GOAL E5 (ACHIEVE (ON A B)))
```

These aren't very exciting either, so I left them out before, but the key is what happens to the GOAL comment on E5. The fun began back when we selected the FACT used to write E5. As the pattern match was done in CAREFUL mode, the program proposer took notes on what he did. The actual match was:

(CODE (ACHIEVE (ON A B)) <u>code</u>)

against:

(CODE (ACHIEVE goal) (UNLESS ...))

where <u>code</u> wanted to be assigned a value. Notice that in the calling pattern, the only constant in (the original) L3 matched against a constant in the FACT was ACHIEVE. This caused the following notation to be made:

(CONSTANT ACHIEVE).

Next, E5 is written, displacing the (ACHIEVE...) in L3. E5 is run, also in CAREFUL mode. The first thing it does is (TEST (ON A B)) which matches (TO (TEST (ON x y))...). This match is also monitored and two more notations are made in HACKER's notebook:

(CONSTANT TEST)
(CONSTANT ON)

Next, the (MAKE (ON A B)) is evaluated. It matches against (TO (MAKE (ON a b))...), causing:

(CONSTANT MAKE)
(CONSTANT ON) - already present

E5 returns, after doing its job successfully, to the program proposer. The program proposer then picks up

(GOAL E5 (ACHIEVE (ON A B)))

a comment he wrote, and goes through it, looking up the notations that have been made on the constants it contains. The only CONSTANT matches were on ACHIEVE and ON; A and B were matched against variables only (all the way down to primitives!). Thus we did nothing which limits this code to work for constants A and B only. (This is also an expository lie; actually there are some restrictions, see Chapter XV, Formal Objects.) Thus it is a good bet that if we substituted anything else for A or B the program would continue to work. The program proposer then formalizes this conjecture by adding the comment:

(NOTICE (ACHIEVE (ON u v)) E5 ((u A) (v B)))

Now it should be clear what is happening. When L4 begins
to run, the program proposer is again called upon to write code for
(ACHIEVE (ON B C)). Now the program proposer, like all
reasonable hackers, is lazy. Before writing code for a specific goal
he checks to see if there is any nice chunk lying around that might
work. It is easy to see that (ACHIEVE (ON B C)) matches
(ACHIEVE (ON u v)), and thus he notices the possible subroutine.
He then extracts the subroutine, by replacing E5 with a call to E5
(from the GOAL comment), and then substitutes u for A and v for
B in the code for E5 (and in all comments on E5), and defines it as a
subroutine, getting the applicability pattern from the NOTICE
comment.

No magic, but then again, it's pretty fancy sleight-of-hand.
Just how far does it go? How general is this method? What bugs
will it produce in more complex cases? I don't know, in general;
much work remains to be done. Just what is happening here?
HACKER generalizes by observing just what he thinks he can get
away with, and then trying it out. Introspectively, it feels like just
what I do when writing a program. I write a special purpose piece
of code, using as general techniques as I can, and then realize that
the same code can be used elsewhere because the techniques
employed in that code do not completely restrict its use to the case
for which it was written.

One bug with the scheme described above is
overvariabilization due to incidental identification of constants. It is
most clearly illustrated by an example in a completely different
domain, that of LOGO turtle geometry problems [Note 16].

Ira Goldstein was observing a child in MATHLAND <Papert
1972a,b>. The child had constructed a procedure for drawing an
equilateral triangle. The general program (not the one the child
had) is:

```
FORWARD :x
RIGHT 120
FORWARD :x
RIGHT 120
FORWARD :x
```

for a triangle of side length x. The child's program, however, was a macro-expansion (it seems) of the general one for side-length 120:

```
FORWARD 120
RIGHT 120
FORWARD 120
RIGHT 120
FORWARD 120
```

The child then decided to change the side length to 90:

```
FORWARD 90
RIGHT 90
FORWARD 90
RIGHT 90
FORWARD 90
```

He was quite surprised at the result! Of course, his problem is that he forgot that some of the 120s are measurements of side-length and others are angular rotation. The accidental equality of the constants, combined with forgetting the semantics of the situation, caused this mild disaster.

That child, and the algorithm described above, have the same bug! They both forgot the semantics of the constants in the code. A better algorithm would not forget, but this is another good "linear" approximation. Various people have suggested schemes by which the semantics of the constants can be remembered for use in later generalization. They essentially amount to commenting each instance of each constant in a program with information about how that constant ended up where it is. Is it the result of a substitution for a variable in a macro expansion? -- if so, where are other instances of that variable? Was it a constant in some macro expanded? etc. Probably some work should be done on this problem.

Both the variabilizer and the COMBINE function described above are available to the critic compiler (see Chapter XI, Critic Compilation), who must generalize on the purpose comments of lines of code which are interacting to cause a bug. In problem 2.1, for example, if the purpose comments of the interacting lines, L3 and L4, are simultaneously variabilized (with respect to the same dictionary -- the correspondence of variables to constants they replace), they become (ACHIEVE (ON a b)) and (ACHIEVE (ON b c)) because, at debugging time, the constants A,

B, and C were unrestricted, in the sense of HACKER's algorithm, and could thus be replaced by variables. Since, however, B appeared in both expressions, it was replaced in both instances by b.

XI. Critic Compilation

When code is written to achieve a conjunctive expression, unless something special is known about the conjuncts, HACKER assumes that they are independently achievable in any order. This assumption may fail in a variety of ways. We have seen that there may be a necessary (but not always sufficient -- see Chapter XIV, Anomalous Situations) order of achievement of subgoals because one subgoal may necessarily destroy another. It may also be the case that subgoals interact so as to fight over some resource, such as space, where, if they can be induced to cooperate, the conflict disappears. Interaction problems can also occur between (cumulative) strategies in heuristic programs, such as the space allocator. As we have seen (in Chapter IX, Types of Bugs), HACKER can distinguish among various types of interaction problems and concoct patches to fix them. As the program patched may be some generally useful subroutine, such as the space allocator, a part of MAKE-ON, the benefit of the debugging can be felt in the solution of future problems; HACKER has learned something. In other cases, however, such as building a three-high tower, the resulting program, even when variabilized, is not of much general use. In fact, HACKER cannot even recognize the fact that (MAKE (AND (ON A B) (ON B C))) is the "same" problem as (MAKE (AND (ON B C) (ON A B))) or that it is a subproblem of (MAKE (AND (ON A B) (ON B C) (ON C D))). It would be painful to have to do the same debugging for each instance of the problem in the four-high tower above, but the essential problem is the same: Structures must be built from the bottom up. How can we make HACKER learn this in general, from one example, so as not to make the same mistake again? The answer is the criticism mechanism wherein programs being written are criticized for interaction bugs and patched before they are released for use. The critics watch over the shoulder of the program proposer. For each line inserted in the new program, the program proposer adds its purpose comments to the data-base. The critics are IF-ADDED methods [Note 10] who trigger on purposes of particular forms. If a critic discovers an error, he leaves a message for the program proposer, who then retracts the proposed program, edits it as directed, and then re-exposes it to the critics. (See Chapter XII, Details of Program Construction, for the types and interpretations of the messages.) In this chapter we examine how critics are constructed from bug descriptions.

For each type of bug in Types of Bugs that HACKER knows how to describe there are specific instructions in Types of Critics (in the form of a macro to expand from the bug description) on how to compile a critic (if any is to be compiled) for an instance of that type of bug. We go through each of the bug types here and describe its associated critic type.

PREREQUISITE-MISSING

PREREQUISITE-MISSING bugs do not form any critics because such bugs are simple to patch; no backtracking in the "real" Blocks World is done because the program has done nothing wrong yet.

PREREQUISITE-CLOBBERS-BROTHER-GOAL

PREREQUISITE-CLOBBERS-BROTHER-GOAL bugs, as in the three-high tower example, however, must compile critics so as to avoid similar troubles in the future. In problem 2.1, the three-high tower problem, the bug was characterized as:

```
(PREREQUISITE-CLOBBERS-BROTHER-GOAL
              AND2 L3 L4 (CLEARTOP B))
```

This means that: "In AND2 the goal of line L3 was clobbered by the achievement of (CLEARTOP B), a prerequisite of L4." This type of bug is specifically a pairwise conflict between ordered brother lines (lines whose purpose comments have the same target) in a conjunctive situation. Thus, to spot this bug at code-writing time we just need to keep an eye open for trying to achieve goals of the form (ON a b) and (ON b c) in that order for the same target. The critic compiler knows this by looking up the instructions for compiling a critic for this kind of bug in Types of Critics (see Overview flowchart, Figure 1):

```
(FACT (CRITIC (PREREQUISITE-CLOBBERS-BROTHER-GOAL
                 prog line1 line2 pre)
       (WATCH-FOR (ORDER (PURPOSE 1line goal1 target)
                         (PURPOSE 2line goal2 target))
                  (PREREQUISITE-CLOBBERS-BROTHER-GOAL
                       current-prog 1line 2line prereq)))
     "AUX" ((DICT ()))
       (CSETQ goal1 (VARIABILIZE (GOAL line1))
              goal2 (VARIABILIZE (GOAL line2))
              prereq (VARIABILIZE pre)) )
```

This instructs the critic compiler as follows: In this general fact, prog=AND2, line1=L3, line2=L4, pre=(CLEARTOP B). Next, goal1 is set to the result of variabilizing the goal of L3, the second slot in its purpose comment. Since the goal of L3 is (ACHIEVE (ON A B)), this yields, by the magic in Chapter X, Generalization and Subroutinization, (ACHIEVE (ON a b)). Next, the goal of L4, (ACHIEVE (ON B C)) is variabilized under the same dictionary, yielding (ACHIEVE (ON b c)), which is given to goal2. Next, (CLEARTOP B) becomes (CLEARTOP b) and is given to prereq. The resulting critic is:

```
(WATCH-FOR
      (ORDER (PURPOSE 1line (ACHIEVE (ON a b)) target)
             (PURPOSE 2line (ACHIEVE (ON b c)) target))
      (PREREQUISITE-CLOBBERS-BROTHER-GOAL current-prog
          1line 2line (CLEARTOP b)))
```

This is further compiled into an IF-ADDED:

```
(IF-ADDED (PURPOSE 1line (ACHIEVE (ON a b)) target)
     (ADD (CLOSURE
          (IF-ADDED (PURPOSE 2line
                            (ACHIEVE (ON b c))
                            target)
              (RECOMMEND
                  (PREREQUISITE-CLOBBERS-BROTHER-GOAL
                        current-prog 1line 2line
                        (CLEARTOP b)))))))
```

which when translated into English from CONNIVER says: If a purpose of the form (PURPOSE 1line (ACHIEVE (ON a b)) target) is added to the data-base, then set up an IF-ADDED to lay in wait for another (PURPOSE 2line (ACHIEVE (ON b c)) target). If one of these comes up, then recommend that the program proposer patch a bug of this type in the program he is currently writing.

STRATEGY-CLOBBERS-BROTHER

In Scenario Section 3 a similar (ordering) bug comes up and is patched:

(STRATEGY-CLOBBERS-BROTHER S6 L7 L8)

For this type of bug, the critic compiler finds:

```
(FACT (CRITIC (STRATEGY-CLOBBERS-BROTHER
                        prog line1 line2)
        (WATCH-FOR (ORDER (PURPOSE 1line goal1 target)
                          (PURPOSE 2line goal2 target))
               (STRATEGY-CLOBBERS-BROTHER
                     current-prog 1line 2line)))
       "AUX" ((DICT ()))
       (CSETQ goal1 (VARIABILIZE (GOAL line1))
              goal2 (VARIABILIZE (GOAL line2)))))
```

Now since (GOAL L7) = (TRY (COMPACT B)) and (GOAL L8) = (TRY (NOT (CLUTTERED B))), the only variabilization made is B==>b. Hence the critic is:

```
(WATCH-FOR
  (ORDER
     (PURPOSE 1line (TRY (COMPACT b)) target)
     (PURPOSE 2line (TRY (NOT (CLUTTERED b))) target))
  (STRATEGY-CLOBBERS-BROTHER current-prog 1line 2line))
```

which further compiles, as in the previous critic, into a nest of IF-ADDEDs.

PREREQUISITE-CONFLICT-BROTHERS

In Scenario Section 4, we encounter a new type of interaction bug. Two objects, A and B, were being placed on C when

HACKER discovered that a fight over space was developing:

```
(PREREQUISITE-CONFLICT-BROTHERS AND11
    ((PLACE-FOR A C) L12)
    ((PLACE-FOR B C) L13))
```

In bugs of this general type there is no reason to expect that there are only two conflicting lines, but there must be at least two for there to be a conflict at all! In this kind of bug, all of the conflicting lines are trying to do the "same" thing. What is it? They are all trying to put something on one object. Thus, to write this critic, we need a way of determining, given several expressions such as (ACHIEVE (ON A C)) and (ACHIEVE (ON B C)), what they have in common, and a way of expressing the result. There is a simple-minded function (described in Chapter X, Generalization and Subroutinization) which attempts to COMBINE a list of expressions by writing one of which they are all an example. If it is given ((PLACE-FOR A C) (PLACE-FOR B C)) it will return (PLACE-FOR {A B} C). So, armed with this COMBINE function, we see that the critic compiler has a very complex fact for compiling critics for this type of bug:

```
(FACT (CRITIC
        (PREREQUISITE-CONFLICT-BROTHERS prog .    con)
        ...))
```

the details of which are hairy and unimportant. In any case, it makes a list of lists of the purpose comments of the complaining lines and their fighting prerequisites:

```
(((PURPOSE L12 (ACHIEVE (ON A C)) AND11)
   (PLACE-FOR A C))
  ((PURPOSE L13 (ACHIEVE (ON B C)) AND11)
   (PLACE-FOR B C)))
```

This is then COMBINEd and variabilized, giving:

```
((PURPOSE {line1 line2} (ACHIEVE (ON {a b} c)) target)
 (PLACE-FOR {a b} c))
```

(The bug type is used for knowing that the line labels and target label could be variabilized.) This is then used to construct the critic:

```
(WATCH-FOR (GIVEN (c t)
                (MORE-THAN-ONE (a line)
                    (PURPOSE line (ACHIEVE (ON a c)) t)))
        (PREREQUISITE-CONFLICT-BROTHERS current-prog
            (EXPAND (line (PLACE-FOR a c)))))
```

This further compiles into an IF-ADDED, which catches every line inserted into a program with purpose (PURPOSE line (ACHIEVE (ON a c)) t). This IF-ADDED keeps a table, containing for every unique such pair, (c t), a set of the associated pairs, (a line). If that set ever gets bigger than one element long, he mails advice to the program proposer saying, "Patch for a bug of type PREREQUISITE-CONFLICT-BROTHERS. The lines and their prerequisites which conflict are in my table as follows: ..."

XII. Details of Program Construction

A program is a method for solving a problem. A line in a program is a step in the solution. Thus, every program has associated with it a goal -- the problem of which it is a solution. Every line has associated with it its purposes -- the parts it plays in the overall problem solution. A line in a program is a main step if by its execution the overall goal is approached. For example, code whose goal is to achieve a conjunction of subgoals may have a step for each conjunct which makes it true. Each of these is a main step. In MAKE-ON, MO1 is the main step because the goal of MAKE-ON, its overall purpose, is (MAKE (ON a b)) and MO1 is the actual call to PUTON. Indeed, before MO1, (ON a b) is false, and after MO1, (ON a b) is true.

Besides the main steps, programs often have auxiliary steps. These are steps which do not directly contribute to the problem solution but rather are written to make the main steps work. An auxiliary step may be inserted to set up for a main step, as in prerequisite insertion, or to serve as a mediator of conflicts between main steps, as in an interface or a double prerequisite. Thus L1 and L5 are auxiliary steps, prerequisite to MO1 in MAKE-ON. Certainly, in complex instances, a prerequisite may have further prerequisites and two prerequisites for the same step may conflict, requiring further interpolation of auxiliary steps. In human programming, most steps are auxiliary.

When a problem (or a subproblem) is attacked, HACKER first looks in the Answer Library for a method whose pattern of applicability matches the problem. If none is found, the program proposer is called. The program proposer first looks around for a chunk of code which might work if subroutinized (and perhaps variabilized -- see Chapter X, Generalization and Subroutinization, for details). If none is found, it is necessary to construct some code. The program proposer advertises for a method to write code for the goal. For example, if the goal is:

(ACHIEVE (NOT (EXISTS (y) (ON y x))))

the program proposer advertises for the answer by invoking methods whose applicability patterns match:

(CODE (ACHIEVE (NOT (EXISTS (y) (ON y x)))) code)

expecting an answer in the form of an assignment of the variable "code" to a program chunk which will perform the desired goal. In this case, a method is found:

(FACT (CODE (ACHIEVE (NOT (EXISTS vars exp)))
           (UNTIL vars (CANNOT (ASSIGN vars exp))
                  (MAKE (NOT exp)))))

Thus, by simple pattern substitution, code is assigned the value:

(UNTIL (y) (CANNOT (ASSIGN (y) (ON y x)))
       (MAKE (NOT (ON y x))))

The program proposer then compiles a one-line program with this as the main step, generating new symbols for the program label and line label:

(HPROG E69
       (LINE L70 (UNTIL (y) (CANNOT (ASSIGN (y) (ON y x)))
                        (MAKE (NOT (ON y x))))))

(where E69 and L70 are the newly generated symbols; the number is incremented by 1 for each new symbol.)

The overall goal and purpose of the line are indicated by comments inserted into the data-base:

(GOAL E69 (ACHIEVE (NOT (EXISTS (y) (ON y x)))))
(PURPOSE L70
         (ACHIEVE (NOT (EXISTS (y) (ON y x))))
         E69)

Since no criticism is made in this case, the original code is displaced by the new code and the program proposer returns to his caller, who then reruns the now-modified expression which started the whole proposal process.

Conjunctive goals, such as (MAKE (AND (ON A B) (ON B C))) do not produce just one main step: How does this work? When the program proposer advertises for:

```
(CODE (MAKE (AND (ON A B) (ON B C))) code)
```

he invokes a general program for AND stuff:

```
(FACT (CODE (function (AND . I)) program)
      (CSETQ program (CONJUNCTION function I)))
```

This program is rather hairy. It knows about all functions (TEST, MAKE, ACHIEVE) of conjunctions of any number of conjuncts (the list is in I). The AND trick takes on the responsibility of code-writing. It constructs the "linear" theory program for the conjunctive expression. It produces one main step per conjunct, whose purpose is to achieve that conjunct, and returns them, with an HPROG and program label it generated, to the program proposer through the variable "code". Thus the trick for AND actually generates, in the case (MAKE (AND (ON A B) (ON B C))) (in problem 2.1),

```
(HPROG AND2
    (LINE L3 (ACHIEVE (ON A B)))
    (LINE L4 (ACHIEVE (ON B C))))
```

which it passes back to the program proposer. The program proposer always checks if the first element of the stuff returned to it is HPROG. If so, it knows that the method generated the program and line labels, and wrote and added the comments. Hence all the program proposer need do is examine his mailbox for criticisms generated by the AND trick, and act on them if there are any, and if not, just displace the calling pattern with the given code and return to the caller. So we see that conjunctive goals lead to programs with multiple main steps. It is important to note here that the linear theory of a conjunction does not always yield an almost-right program -- one that can be debugged to achieve the conjunction. A good example is that of the ARCH:

```
(ACHIEVE (AND (ON A B) (ON A C)))
```

The error is a combination of a DOUBLE-MOVE and a PROTECTION-VIOLATION. I have spent weeks (literally!) trying to understand how to "debug" the linear theory program for this goal but I have not come up with a satisfactory solution.

Perhaps some problems depend so strongly upon the interactions
between subgoals that the linear-theory solution is not a sufficient
starting point. Currently, therefore, HACKER can only construct
programs for which the linear theory is almost-right.

Now what about criticism? When problem 2.2, (MAKE
(AND (ON A B) (ON C D) (ON B C))), is run, the experience of
debugging 2.1 has left around a critic (see Chapter XI, Critic
Compilation):

```
(WATCH-FOR
    (ORDER (PURPOSE 1line (ACHIEVE (ON a b)) t)
           (PURPOSE 2line (ACHIEVE (ON b c)) t))
    (PREREQUISITE-CLOBBERS-BROTHER-GOAL
        current-prog 1line 2line (CLEARTOP b)))
```

The trick for AND compiles, in its stupid way:

```
(HPROG AND71
    (LINE L72 (ACHIEVE (ON A B)))
    (LINE L73 (ACHIEVE (ON C D)))
    (LINE L74 (ACHIEVE (ON B C))))
```

After compiling this, it starts reading it:

```
(GOAL AND71
        (MAKE (AND (ON A B) (ON C D) (ON B C))))
(PURPOSE L72 (ACHIEVE (ON A B)) AND71)
```

The critic perks up his ears (1line=L72, a=A, b=B, t=AND71) and sets
a trap for things of the form:

```
(PURPOSE 2line (ACHIEVE (ON B c)) AND71).
```

The reader continues reading:

```
(PURPOSE L73 (ACHIEVE (ON C D)) AND71)
```

Another trap is set, this time for:

```
(PURPOSE 2line (ACHIEVE (ON D c)) AND71)
```

The reader continues:

```
(PURPOSE L74 (ACHIEVE (ON B C)) AND71)
```

The first trap snaps with 2line=L74 and c=C. The advice is mailed:

```
(PATCH (PREREQUISITE-CLOBBERS-BROTHER-GOAL
              AND71 L72 L74 (CLEARTOP B)))
```

Also, another trap is set for:

```
(PURPOSE 2line (ACHIEVE (ON C c)) AND71)
```

The AND trick now returns to the program proposer, who is chagrined to find the warning in his mailbox. He executes it; but it turns itself into:

```
(BEFORE L74 L72)
```

via:

```
(FACT (PATCH (PREREQUISITE-CLOBBERS-BROTHER-GOAL
                        prog line1 line2 prereq)
          (BEFORE line2 line1)))
```

The BEFORE adds itself to the data-base and sets a flag in the program proposer to sort the program. The program is re-sorted, yielding:

```
(HPROG AND71
    (LINE L74 (ACHIEVE (ON B C)))
    (LINE L72 (ACHIEVE (ON A B)))
    (LINE L73 (ACHIEVE (ON C D))))
```

This is still not quite right, but the old traps are deactivated, and the program is re-aired. In this iteration L73 is moved up before L74, fixing the bug, and only now is the code released to be run, correctly the first time! Initially, there is only one criterion built into the system which causes programs to be ordered: Prerequisites must come before the lines which are the targets of their purposes. To enforce this, every program is sorted at least once before it is released.

XIII. The Protection Mechanism

Essential to the ability to debug programs is the ability to know when a program is misbehaving. As in programming systems used by people, bugs in HACKER's programs may manifest themselves by a primitive complaining about the task it is asked to perform, as in UNSATISFIED-PREREQUISITE type bugs. A program may fail to do its job without arousing any primitive. The primitives may be asked to perform legal manipulations, but the overall result may be incorrect. This may be the case if either some piece of code fails to do its job or a nasty interaction undoes the work done by previously executed code. The protection mechanism is the method by which HACKER is made aware of these more subtle diseases.

Human programmers, who are not provided with anything more closely resembling the protection mechanism than the address stop switch on the computer console (or the MAR interrupt of ITS [Note 17]), often write special debugging aids into their programs. These usually amount to scattered tests for impossible (inconsistent with the assumed state) situations. Carl Hewitt has proposed a uniform method, called Intentions, of including such tests in a higher-level language (see [Note 9], PLANNER). He has also proposed that an extension of address stop, the Monitors, be included in higher-level languages. Periodic tests, or Intentions, are useful in verifying that a program is working correctly. If, however, a program fails, and this is noticed by the failure of some test which was expected to succeed, we still have not found out why it failed. If the test was true at some previous time, then we know that it was made untrue by some code executed between that time and the present. Monitors, on the other hand, make it possible to trap all accesses to and modifications of a data structure. Thus bugs which involve clobbering data can be caught *in flagrante delicto*.

HACKER's protection mechanism is a combination of the ideas of Intentions and Monitors under the unifying concept of "the chronological scope" of a goal. (The idea that goals have scopes was planted in my head by Marvin Minsky.) This is directly related to

HACKER's belief that each step of a program has a (at least one) purpose. That purpose may be either to contribute to the overall purpose of the program, or to provide some part of the correct conditions for later steps. Thus, the purposes of a step in a program are not just its Intentions, the goals which can be assumed to be true after the step is run, but also the target users of each of the goals achieved. Hence a program is operating correctly, in that it accurately reflects the intent of the programmer, only when each step achieves those goals that the programmer intended it to, and each of those goals remains true at least until the steps which depend upon its being true are run (or the end of the program block if this step is a contributor to the purpose of the program).

The protection mechanism in HACKER programs is armed by the PURPOSE comments associated with each line of code written by HACKER. Thus, in the program MAKE-ON:

```
(TO (MAKE (ON a b))
     (HPROG MAKE-ON
          (LINE L1 ...  )
          (LINE L5 ...  )
          (LINE MO1 (PUTON a b))))
```

the comments are:

```
(PURPOSE L1 (ACHIEVE (CLEARTOP a)) MO1)
(PURPOSE L5 (ACHIEVE (PLACE-FOR a b)) MO1)
(PURPOSE MO1 (MAKE (ON a b)) MAKE-ON)
```

The second position in a PURPOSE is the "source" line. When executed, the source must perform the service indicated by the third position for the "target", the fourth position. Since the effect of (ACHIEVE (CLEARTOP a)) is to make (CLEARTOP a) true, we say that (CLEARTOP a) is protected over the scope L1 to MO1. Similarly, (ON a b) is protected over the scope MO1 to (the end of) MAKE-ON. In this case, since MO1 is last in MAKE-ON, no trouble can happen. If an expression is protected over some scope, then if we are running in CAREFUL mode, it is checked for truth at the beginning of the scope (an error will result if it isn't true) and during the scope an error will result if anything happens to make the expression untrue.

How is this implemented? At the entry to every HPROG a CONNIVER context (see [Note 14]) is pushed and rebound. Thus a

HACKER program has a data-base structure which reflects the dynamic structure of the program. This is in addition to the chronological structure mentioned in Chapter IX. After a line, say Ll, is run, its purpose comments are retrieved and activated by adding to the dynamic (not chronological!) context:

(ACTIVE L1 (ACHIEVE (CLEARTOP A)) M01)

where A (say) is the value of a. This invokes the protection mechanism by means of IF-ADDED methods:

(IF-ADDED (ACTIVE line (ACHIEVE exp) target)
      ...   )

or

(IF-ADDED (ACTIVE line (MAKE exp) target)
      ...   )

These test the truth of exp, and if it passes the test, exp is protected by adding (to the current context frame):

(PROTECT exp) e.g. (PROTECT (CLEARTOP A))

Later, when MOl is about to be run, all items (in the current context frame) of the form:

(ACTIVE line goal M01)

are removed from the current context frame because they have served their purpose. IF-REMOVEDs are used to clean up and remove the protections which were inserted as a consequence of the particular active comment. As the dynamic protection context is popped when the HPROG returns, the protection of (ON A B) generated by activating the comment on MOl disappears.

Whenever a change is made to the world model (the chronological context) a test is made to see if any protection has been violated. All currently protected expressions are fetched from the dynamic context and tested in the world model. An error results if one is found to be untrue. Thus HACKER runs <u>very</u> slowly in CAREFUL mode.

PROTECTED? is implemented as follows: A hypothetical world model is created with the changes indicated by the negation of the argument to PROTECTED? made. This requires IF-ADDEDs and IF-REMOVEDs to produce a consistent result. The protected expressions are then checked out in the hypothetical world and if any have been violated, PROTECTED? returns TRUE.

XIV. Anomalous Situations

As we have seen in Chapter IX, Types of Bugs, I have worked out in detail the underlying causes of only a few types of bugs. Unfortunately, it turns out that this classification is not sufficient for even all of the bugs encountered in Blocks World problems. Bugs may become manifest to the error system for which none of the known classifications is appropriate.

One approach to solving this problem is to attempt to extend the number of bug types for which classifications, patches, and perhaps generalizations are known. We can hope that by diligent effort we can eventually classify all bugs that can come up, and understand them sufficiently to know what kinds of patches to prescribe for each type. I feel that this approach is very promising, however large the task may seem now. We in Artificial Intelligence have often been pleasantly surprised at the remarkably small "size of infinity" -- that is, the manageably small number of features required to classify what initially seems to be a horrible problem.

Another approach is to attempt to create a more general theory of debugging -- one in which the properties of bugs are derived from more general principles, and from which all bug types can be derived. I am more skeptical of this approach. I expect that it will become profitable only after we see a more exhaustive survey of bugs in at least a few distinct domains.

In any case, until we have a complete functional taxonomy of bugs, it is necessary that problem solvers be provided with ways of dealing with these anomalous situations -- that is, error situations for which no general classification fits. Even if the problem solver is at a loss to debug and patch (hence learn about) this kind of problem, he must be able to muddle through, however inefficiently, and provide the user with a solution. In this chapter we will examine how HACKER attempts to lose gracefully in some situations which to him are anomalous.

Sometimes, one way to make a problem go away, if it isn't so critical that it has to be fixed immediately, is to ignore it. In the case of DOUBLE-MOVE manifestations, which are really warnings rather than clear errors, if the situation is not a clear-cut case of a known bug, the error system just notes the state of the performance program for use in debugging if a serious bug appears later, and returns control to the interrupted performance program. In Scenario Section 5 (Chapter VIII) several such false alarms are dismissed. The error system, to be sure that nothing is missed, is really rather twitchy in CAREFUL mode, and things may seem to be in a bad way even if they are proceeding smoothly.

If the manifestation is more serious, and real mischief is afoot, HACKER cannot just run away from the problem. Suppose, for example, that HACKER has already learned the lessons of Scenario Section 2, that structures are to be built from the bottom up, and he is presented with the problem (first noticed by Allen Brown):

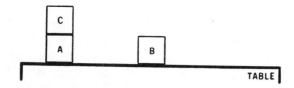

Statement: (MAKE (AND (ON A B) (ON B C)))

Certainly it is true that in any problem of this form, B must be placed on C before A is placed on B because B cannot be moved with A on it. Hence HACKER compiles the program:

```
(HPROG AND40
    (LINE L41 (ACHIEVE (ON B C)))
    (LINE L42 (ACHIEVE (ON A B))))
```

But notice the problem: If B is placed on C first, then when A is to be moved (to put on B), A must be CLEARTOP, requiring the removal of C and thus the removal of B. A very nasty PROTECTION-VIOLATION. It's a terrible pity, but as we see in 2.1, A cannot be put on B first. What does HACKER do?

The error system attempts to classify the manifestation into one of the known underlying causes. I shall first show why this does not fit any of the known groups. A process model is prepared (see Figure 12) as usual. The classifier looks at this model and asks (question 3 in Chapter IX, Types of Bugs):

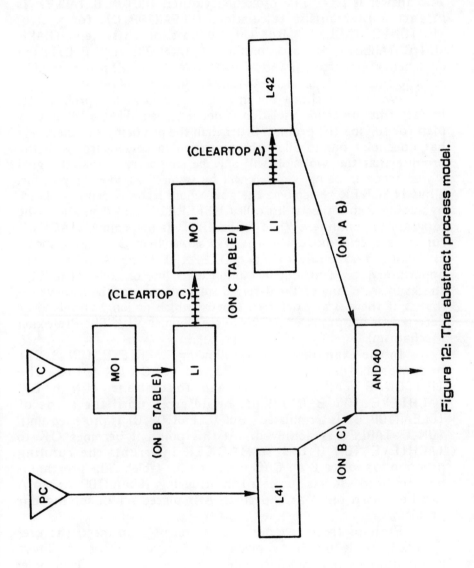

Figure 12: The abstract process model.

Is the protection violator a prerequisite calculation for a step whose purpose is to satisfy a brother goal to the one violated?

The answer is NO: The protection violator, (PUTON B TABLE), is in fact a prerequisite calculation, (CLEARTOP C), for a step, (PUTON C TABLE). But the purpose of this step, (MAKE (ON C TABLE)), is not a brother of (ACHIEVE (ON B C)), the goal being violated. In fact, (MAKE (ON C TABLE)) is part of a prerequisite calculation, (CLEARTOP A), for a brother goal.

We are also clearly not in a strategy conflict like problem 3.5. In fact, this protection violation is not classified. HACKER has no plan for solving the problem better than the one being executed. He has no choice but to allow the protection to be violated, with the promise that the violation will only be temporary -- that the goal whose scope is being violated will be restored as soon as possible. Thus HACKER remembers the goal whose scope is being violated, by adding it to a special list called DEFERRED, and then allows the program to continue. When DEFERRED is non-empty, HACKER runs in a special mode which is even slower than CAREFUL mode. He wants very badly to make DEFERRED empty, so at every opportunity, say finishing execution of a line of code, HACKER checks to see if any of the deferred subgoals can now be achieved -- that is, if there is any deferred subgoal which no longer needs to be deferred (is not protected against -- see Chapter XIII, The Protection Mechanism).

In the example we were following, (ACHIEVE (ON B C)) becomes a deferred subgoal, and HACKER allows the (PUTON B TABLE) to proceed to clobber (ON B C). (ACHIEVE (ON B C)) must be deferred until the scope of (CLEARTOP C) is terminated. But (CLEARTOP C) is protected until (ON C TABLE) is achieved. At this point, it becomes OK to (ACHIEVE (ON B C)) so HACKER interrupts the running program to replace B on C (C is now on the table). The program is now resumed. It has succeeded in achieving (CLEARTOP A), so A can be placed on B as expected. A is placed on B, solving our problem.

Perhaps there is more to this process than meets the eye? Currently, while in deferred mode, double moves are ignored. There are indications that much can be learned by studying the double-move structure of a problem-solving process in deferred mode. Drew McDermott has suggested that a bug-type abstraction process might result from such a study. In any case, this technique of deferring violated subgoals is very general. Computer programs written by people are often forced to save the contents of an active register to be restored later because some computation to be done between the save and restore may clobber that register. In the Blocks World it saves the day in many other situations. For example, consider problem 3.6, with the added constraint: (PROTECT (ON D C)). In this case, we cannot make room for A on B without pushing C. This, however, requires that D be removed from C. It is necessary to replace D before the problem is completed. The protection violation causes deferment of (ON D C) which is re-established as soon as C is pushed. This is actually a rather elegant solution.

XV. Formal Objects

This chapter was reserved for the end because the technique illustrated herein is not in the mainstream of HACKER development and no effort was made to push it to its logical conclusions. I believe that the formal object technique is potentially a powerful one in the "bag of tricks" of the problem-solver writer. Its present incarnation, however, is rather immature and needs further development.

I promised to explain how HACKER knew, in the expansion of CLEARTOP in Scenario Section 1, when confronted with the problem:

(MAKE (EXISTS (z) (AND (NOT (= z a)) (ON y z)))),

to CHOOSE z from the set of SURFACEs. The truth is, I lied; HACKER did not, at the indicated point, know how to CHOOSE z. What did he do?

One thing that can be done, which is what HACKER does, is to apply the "wishful thinking" technique. The trick is to assume that the choice can and has been made, and then proceed in the hope that we'll find out soon enough. Specifically, the FACT used in writing code for (MAKE (EXISTS (z) goal)) really expands into:

```
(CHOOSE (z) ((UNKNOWN z))
    (TEST (POSSIBLE goal))
    (MAKE goal))
```

UNKNOWN is a very special selector which assigns to z a new symbol (uniquely generated and having no properties except that it is formally unknown) whose purpose is to collect information and assumptions made about the expected contents of z while the code using z is run. Associated with the formal object is the process which created it -- the state of the interpreter at the time it was chosen. Thus, when sufficient information is acquired to clarify the situation and determine the choice, or a choice is forced, HACKER can find his way back to the place where the patch is to be made.

Let us assume that z is assigned the formal unknown F. The program then continues into the test which expands and runs as described in Chapter IV. Certainly F is not equal to B (the value of a), and no information is picked up here. Then (NOT (PROTECTED? (NOT (ON A F)))) is evaluated (A is the value of y). The Protection Mechanism finds no reason to fear (ON A F) and here we pick up nothing either. (A more clever mechanism would note that F is something which A can be ON.) Thus F seems to pass the choice test, and we go to (MAKE (ON y z)) where y=A and z=F. A recursive call is made to MAKE-ON. Inside MAKE-ON a=A and b=F. The recently inserted (and currently under modification) line L1 cannot assign y such that (ON y A); A has a clear top, so execution proceeds to MO1 which tries to (PUTON A F). Now PUTON is a primitive operator and, by convention, HACKER primitives must declare, upon entry, the type of each argument. PUTON declares: (OBJECT A) and (SURFACE F). These declarations are just added to the data-base when HACKER is in CAREFUL mode. Now PUTON actually attempts to go through the action of putting A on F. That requires PUTON to figure out where on F A should be placed. But F is discovered not to have a size or shape. PUTON becomes unhappy at this point and calls the error system with the message:

(BUG FUNNY-THING F)

This indicates that the complainer, PUTON, is unhappy with F because it was lacking a property that PUTON expects on F's property list. The error system now investigates the origin of F and determines that F is a formal unknown. Since the error system also has access to the creator of F, the CHOOSE, it passes control back to the creator, giving him a pointer to the complainer. The creator, CHOOSE, looks into the data-base of the complainer and sees that PUTON expected (SURFACE F). Since PUTON cannot proceed with F unknown, this complaint cannot be ignored, and SURFACE is taken to be the UNKNOWN selector. CHOOSE then determines that y was the variable which was assigned F so the selection argument is forced to be (SURFACE y). It is so clobbered. Then CHOOSE restarts itself, this time selecting a real surface, TABLE, for y, and hence successfully terminating.

XVI. Conclusions

By now you are probably convinced that HACKER can solve toy problems in the Blocks World, and even that his performance improves with practice in that domain. So what?!

A. The basic concepts behind HACKER

I feel that HACKER elucidates the nature of several Powerful Ideas, ideas which are basic to effective problem solving. I certainly do not claim that these ideas are exhaustive, or even sufficient for the Blocks World. Others with different points of view may find a different set of Powerful Ideas in HACKER or see some that I have overlooked. I do feel, however, that we would be hard pressed to find an area of significant intellectual attainment in which these ideas lack power.

1. The bug

We usually consider a bug at best an annoyance. We rarely think of one as illustrating an important point (except as a counterexample), and we almost never think of "BUG" as a powerful idea. This is rather surprising, as a large portion of a computer scientist's time is spent debugging. It is even more surprising when we realize that at least several professions (outside the computer field) are largely concerned with debugging. We have physicians for debugging our bodies, auto mechanics for our cars, and psychiatrists for our emotions. Contrary to popular belief about mathematicians, scientists, and engineers, complete formal theories do not usually arise fully formed and well understood. They are usually arrived at by a painful process of successive approximation and refinement. Perhaps the difficulty is cultural. We are taught in school that mistakes are abhorrent and that only success should be studied. Even as professionals, we rarely see papers published about negative results. Problem-solving programs have so far reflected this prejudice of their authors [Note 18]. They are thought of as mechanisms to search some "space of solutions" for solutions to problems. Much thought has been given to "efficiently" searching this space. Modern work on knowledge-based systems is usually aimed at providing special-purpose problem solvers with special-purpcse knowledge designed to guide them so that only the most plausible paths are investigated. Very little thought has gone into directing what happens when the problem solver finds itself at a dead end; usually an automatic depth-first search mechanism is provided for such contingencies with the hope that the positive guidance will be sufficiently strong to prevent combinatorial explosion.

HACKER, however, considers wrong choices to be just as interesting as correct choices. The philosophy here is that rather than ignoring a bug in the search for a correct answer, understanding it is the source of power over it. It is often the case that the "basic idea" of a proposed solution will work if we can only isolate the problem and patch it.

Bugs are so important that it is useful to classify them and give the classes names. In real world problem solving we often give names to important classes of bugs. In electrical engineering, for example, one class of bug is "instability". It may be manifest as "thermal runaway" or "spurious oscillation" in an amplifier. The underlying cause is "positive feedback", and there are several possible cures (patches) which may be applied: "negative feedback", or "isolation", for example. Debugging is only valuable, however, if the results of the debugging can be used to guide the future operation of the problem solver. Somehow, the results of the debugging operation must be summarized and made available to the control structure to be useful. We must somehow be able to "learn" from mistakes.

2. The relationship between learning and problem solving

In a sense, even an elementary exponential-search problem solver learns during the course of solving a particular problem. It remembers (perhaps by forgetting them!) those paths which have proven unfruitful so that they will not be repeatedly explored. (Many predicate-calculus theorem provers lack even this rudimentary skill.) There have been attempts to improve the performance of problem solvers by the introduction of "memory". These efforts have ranged from rote memory of the results of all searches made (so that no specific search is duplicated) [Note 19] through tree-pruning algorithms such as alpha-beta in two person games, to some rather sophisticated attempts to generalize successful lines for use in future subproblems [Note 20]. In the last case the resulting "plans" are of only limited utility because their application is carefully limited to subproblems satisfying conditions which guarantee correct operation of the stored plans -- bugs are not allowed. In HACKER, bugs are encouraged by ruthless generalization. The resulting subroutines, however bug-ridden, are applicable to all situations even vaguely resembling the ones for which they were written. The debugging process is called into play to determine how the existing routine may be modified to fit the new situation if a bug turns up. The results of debugging are summarized and hence remembered (or learned) as the patch concocted to fix the bug. In some cases, the bug discovered is also generalized and remembered as a critic, a daemon which prevents the construction of a program having that kind of bug.

Learning of procedures and critics of the kind of generality done by HACKER is quite amenable to cumulative procedural learning -- across problem boundaries. This skill acquisition is more project-oriented than problem-oriented. An important limitation of HACKER (which I believe is shared by people) makes it necessary to carefully plan the training sequence. This is because the actual problem-solving power of the bug classifier is limited.

3. Separation of and isolation of bugs

Most interesting (and difficult) bugs result from unanticipated interference between steps in a proposed solution of a problem. If HACKER can recognize any one such bug (if it has a description of that kind of bug) it can be expected to be able to cope with situations where that kind of bug pops up. There is a second-order kind of interference, however, which HACKER (and most humans, I believe) cannot handle. This occurs when there is a bug manifestation which is the result of more than one underlying cause, or when the manifestation of one bug hides (or cancels) the manifestation of another. Even an individual bug manifestation can have its significance confused by its occurring in an overly complex situation.

I am fond of an example from electronic circuit design. If we ask a student who is just learning about the appropriate way to bias a transistor so as to yield an amplifier which is thermally stable, to design and construct a tuned linear amplifier for 50 MHz operation, we should expect him to have a very tough time, even assuming that he is a whiz at linear circuit theory and thus should have no trouble with the input and output tanks. The difficulty is that at 50 MHz a whole new class of instabilities rears its ugly head. Besides the dc instability which he is currently learning to cope with, at 50 MHz the internal capacitances in the transistor become very significant, so positive feedback through that path -- leading to non-linear operation (at best, and most subtly), spurious oscillation, and even thermal runaway -- becomes an important factor. I would be exceedingly impressed with a student who could sort out the two different underlying causes of the instability (the manifestation) and come up with the appropriate patches, one in the dc bias network, and the other the introduction of a neutralization circuit.

In HACKER a similar kind of situation can occur if we try to give him a problem which has the possibility of interlocking bugs. Say, for example, that HACKER has not yet learned about the ordering of towers (Section 2) or the planning for simultaneous use of space (Section 4) and we give him the problem

(MAKE (AND (ON B C) (ON A D) (ON C D)))

where A, B, and C are on the table and D is just large enough to hold A and C.

First, B is put on C, then A on D. Next C has to be put on D. But B is on C and an attempt is made to remove it, leading to a protection violation. The bug is analyzed and it is decided that the program is to be reordered so C is placed on D before B is placed on C. The program is patched and the world is restored to the beginning. The program is rerun. Now C is placed in the middle of D and B is placed on it. A cannot be placed on D because C is in the way. Perhaps C should be pushed over, but that involves removing B, another protection violation. This one is anomalous (cannot be classified as one of the currently known bug types). HACKER can muddle through, solving the problem in Anomalous mode; however, the secondary bug casts grave doubt on the validity of the first patch (which was correct). This patch and its critic survive, however. Furthermore, the secondary bug, by being anomalous, masked the double-move of C, and hence the learning about planning ahead.

Thus, to make learning reasonably possible, it is important to construct a good training sequence. HACKER points at one important criterion for such a training sequence (for people as well as HACKER) -- that the bugs be isolated and separated. Perhaps this might be an important principle in curriculum design.

A good problem solver (say an intelligent human), when stymied by a difficult problem, often "fools around" with easier related problems before reattacking the hard one head-on. If asked about what he is doing, he might reply, "I am feeling out the lay of the land". I submit that he is creating related problems in the hope that solving them will isolate some of the bugs in his approach which by their confluence have impeded his progress. Creating one's own training sequences is in fact an important part of intellectual creativity.

In many hard problems, the subproblems which are generated form a sufficient training sequence. HACKER takes full advantage of that kind of fortuitous learning. In other cases, like the one just described, HACKER cannot separate out the problems. Perhaps an important next step in the development of problem-solving systems would be a thorough investigation of the problem of effective exploratory behavior. One shallow suggestion, indicated by the example above, is that in the case of a conjunction of subgoals in which trouble is encountered, one should first try solving the subproblems individually, then in pairs, etc. Such a self-generated training sequence would bring out each bug separately (in the case shown) and thus be exactly what is needed to fix the confusion.

4. Planning and "Linear Theories"

As indicated previously, most interesting (and difficult) bugs result from unanticipated interference between steps in a proposed problem solution. Why is there such unanticipated interference between steps? This takes us back to the fact that we require extensibility of our problem solver. Extensibility, however, demands modularity of the representation of the knowledge from which the solutions of problems are proposed. Modularity is the restriction that an element of knowledge be self-contained, that it not be dependent upon other coexisting elements of knowledge. If it is necessary to propose a multi-step solution to a problem from such knowledge elements which do not know about each other, then the only way that the proposer can operate is to propose a solution in which the steps are assumed not to interact. Only after we have such a "linear theory plan" can we then bring to bear other knowledge to refine the plan to a working program. This other knowledge can be explicit and specific, hence efficiently applicable for avoiding bugs (critics), or general and expensive to apply (as is debugging information).

This idea of "linear approximation" turns out to be a powerful complexity-limiting device, which is as important in the history of science as it is in solving individual problems. The key is to make believe, say in the case of a conjunction problem, that the conjuncts are independent and they won't interact. This leads to a plausible plan for solving the problem, the sequential independent solution of the conjuncts, in the hope that the results are additive (superposition). Often the linear theory works and we are done. In other cases, the "linear theory" has a bug and interactions must be debugged, but the mode of failure is often indicative of the kind of interaction causing the trouble, and thus the kind of patch or elaboration of the theory needed. In some cases (as in ARCH) the linear theory doesn't help. In those cases, the conjunction cannot be broken up into its individual conjuncts but rather must be achieved as a unit. Perhaps in these cases more subtle analysis of the linear theory would be fruitful? -- perhaps something can be done by merging plans?

The linearization approach is often used in synthetic problem solving. Going back to electronic circuit design, consider the design of a stereo high-fidelity amplifier. Such a device consists of three subdevices, an amplifier module for each channel and a power supply. The two amplifiers are identical. On first pass, the engineer will design the parts separately. He will design a high-fidelity amplifier module, and a power supply capable of supporting two of them. An engineer, being skilled, has a critic that recognizes a possible interaction bug -- the amplifiers are coupled through the power supply (any realizable supply has a non-zero output impedance) leading to some loss of stereo separation. (A beginner would probably build the circuit and then discover the bug, make a patch and compile a critic.) The situation can be improved (the channels better isolated) by lowering the impedance of the power supply. This can be achieved by the introduction of a voltage regulator circuit which actively (by negative feedback) attempts to maintain a constant output voltage of the power supply. This further necessitates increasing the overall ratings of the power supply to give the voltage regulator room to maneuver.

B. The basic mechanisms in HACKER

HACKER is a rather complex problem-solving program built from many diverse mechanisms. In this section I will attempt to summarize the structure of HACKER and point out the most important of these mechanisms. One mechanism which deserves a name is the overall structure and flow of control as described in Chapter III as well as here, the HACKER-Structure.

The overall intention is a skill-acquiring problem solver to which knowledge may be added in a modular fashion. Skill is acquired by remembering and using the answers to previously solved problems and remembering and avoiding the traps previously fallen into. In general, a solution to a problem is a sequence of actions (a program) which, when executed, effects the solution. The sequence of actions for a particular problem depends upon the statement of the problem and the situation (context) in which the problem is posed. In order that such an answer be applicable to new problems in new situations it must be ruthlessly generalized and stored, indexed by the pattern which is a generalized statement of the problem for which it was written. The collection of such generalized answers is called the Answer Library. The scheme by which answers are generalized is detailed in Chapter X.

The hope is that a problem with a "similar" statement to one already solved will have a similar solution. Thus, when an answer from the Answer Library is applied to a new problem which matches its pattern of applicability, it should (at least almost) work. Generalizations are made, however, very ruthlessly, so subroutines are often used in situations very different from those prevailing when they were written. Bugs occur because proposed answers often take advantage of special properties of the situations for which the answers were written. These bugs may be manifest in a variety of ways. A primitive may complain that its prerequisites are unsatisfied or the protection mechanism (see Chapter XIII) may discover that a result which has been established is being clobbered before the need for that result has expired. Bugs may also be indicated by certain aesthetic principles of the problem domain being violated.

A debugging system is provided to make it possible to use an almost correct solution to a problem. If successful, debugging results in a patch to the solution which extends it to the current situation. The buggy program serves as a higher level "plan" for the "correct" solution which replaces it. Thus the patches "improve" the subroutines in the Answer Library by making them applicable to the more general situations for which they are advertised to work by their applicability patterns. Knowledge of successful problem solutions is summarized and remembered in usable form as subroutines and patches to them in the Answer Library.

The debugging system first attempts to classify a bug (see Chapter IX). The bug classifier examines the manifestation and attempts to determine the underlying cause of the bug. This is accomplished by matching a teleological model of the process in which the bug became manifest against a set of prototypical bug types. The teleological model is constructed from the process structure (stacks) and the comments associated with the code when it was constructed. These comments specify, for each line of code, why and how it was constructed. Every line has (at least one) purpose. A purpose has a lexical scope and a goal. It states that the purpose of the line in question is to achieve the goal specified because the line which is the target of the lexical scope needs that goal achieved. In the process resulting from running a program, the lexical scope of a purpose becomes a chronological scope (the goal is needed until the target line is encountered). The protection mechanism is implemented by activating daemons which protect the goal of a purpose over its chronological scope.

If the manifest bug can be classified, and the underlying cause determined, a patch can be concocted. Often it is the case that a whole class of such bugs can be recognized before they ever become manifest. In such cases a critic is compiled (see Chapter XI), which watches as new answers are written. The critic will catch bugs of the type for which it was compiled at the time the code is constructed, and cause them to be patched before they ever run. A critic is a way of summarizing and avoiding traps previously fallen into. The group of critics which represent knowledge learned from debugging is called the Critic's Gallery.

New code is written whenever a problem appears for which no current answer is applicable. The code proposer draws upon two banks of facts called the Blocks World Knowledge Library and the Programming Techniques Library. Because of the intent to keep the Blocks World Knowledge Library facts independent of each other, and hence modular, interactions between steps, a common cause of bugs, are ignored by the code proposer. Thus, unless appropriate critics are around to prevent them, the code proposer can often produce buggy code. It is the code proposer who writes the comments specifying the purpose of each line of code, however, so that the debugging system can work out any troubles. The facts used by the code proposer are stated as <u>pattern-invoked</u> <u>macros</u> and new code is written by macro-expansion.

C. Limitations of HACKER

It would be nice to be able to say that all it takes to make HACKER perform in a new domain is to replace (or preferably augment) the Blocks World Knowledge Library with a library of facts and definitions appropriate to the new domain, and to supply a few new domain-specific primitives (appropriately documented as to their purposes and prerequisites in the domain-specific knowledge library). Unfortunately, there are several major impediments in this direction:

1. The more general problem-solving knowledge found in the Programming Techniques Library, Types of Bugs, Types of Patches, and Types of Critics, is at best incomplete. HACKER knows nothing about such important general programming worlds as data structures and numerical methods, and the classes of bugs, etc., for such worlds. I believe that this kind of knowledge could be added to HACKER's repertoire, though the process is long and arduous. This kind of knowledge, unlike the Blocks World Knowledge Library, is not very modular. For each new kind of programming structure there is a set of bug types to be classified, and their associated generalized patches and critics to be worked out. I am sure, for example, that the Bug Classifier has inadequate problem-solving power for any real extension, and that many different bug types would have to be examined carefully before we would begin to understand the real requirements. As it is now, understanding and formalizing one new bug type is an enormous effort.

2. It is not yet clear just how hard it is to formalize the domain-specific knowledge necessary to write the analogue of a Blocks World Knowledge Library for another domain. I feel sure that it must be easier than writing an expert program for that domain because the facts required for such a library are more modular. Indeed, the expert needs to know (in its implicit, distributed way) all of the "facts" which make up such a library. In addition, the expert must have, embodied in its structure, the important interactions between the facts, again distributed as necessary. What would appear as one "fact" in a knowledge library would appear in many

places in an expert program. In an expert, specifications of the interactions themselves, like how to resolve spatial conflicts (see Chapter VII), would never appear explicitly, as in HACKER, but would be implicitly used in any place where such a conflict could arise.

In summary, I believe that this limitation is more a matter of conjecture than reality.

3. A more fundamental problem than either of the preceding two is that HACKER lacks an important kind of overview capability. I, as a programmer, usually find myself doing the kind of thing which HACKER seems to be good at. I extend a program by an evolutionary process, "debugging" it to work in new situations for which it was not originally intended, adding new features, and including new ideas. Sometimes, however, I find myself doing what seems to be qualitatively different. I look at the program and say to myself, "This is getting to be an ugly kludge and it is time to rewrite it." I then proceed to understand the program as written as thoroughly as possible and then reorganize the whole structure into a new and more pleasant form. I am being deliberately vague on this issue because I don't understand it, but I know that HACKER just doesn't have anything like that ability.

D. Directions for future research

All through this document I have tried to point out where HACKER was inadequate and how he might be improved. In particular, people should:

1. Extend HACKER-like problem-solving techniques to other worlds.
2. Study more different classes of bugs.
3. Develop a language for description of bug types based on whatever is needed in the way of problem-solving power in the bug classification stuff.

A world which is considerably more rich than the Blocks World but which seems exceptionally accessible at this time is the world of electronic circuit design. I think that it is not inconceivable that a program could be written using HACKER-like techniques which would learn to design transistor amplifiers on a training sequence composed of problem sets from the electrical engineering core curriculum.

I also hope that this research will stimulate interest in those problems which I haven't begun to attack but have only alluded to:

1. The problem of purposeful exploratory behavior.
2. The problem of seemingly global overview and reorganization.
3. Problems for which the linear theory answer is not a good first approximation.

Notes

1. From "Webster's Seventh New Collegiate Dictionary", G.&C. Merriam Co. (1965)

2. Various versions of HACKER have been implemented, no one of which has all of the features described in this document. No difficulty is foreseen in a complete implementation, however, and one is expected.

3. The Blocks World has been intensively investigated by people interested in problem solving because of its apparent simplicity and interesting structure. Terry Winograd <Winograd 1971> used it as the subject of his semantic model in his natural language understanding system. Recently, Scott Fahlman <Fahlman 1973> has constructed a problem solver which shows remarkable expertise in the Blocks World. Carl Hewitt <Hewitt 1972> has used the Blocks World for several examples of Procedural Abstraction by protocol analysis.

4. For one man's opinion about "Automatic Programming" and related issues, look at Balzer's <Balzer 1972> report. Besides trying to understand all of the issues involved, Balzer provides an extensive bibliography, a summary of each approach, and a list of people involved in the field.

5. This approach is typified by the work of Waldinger and Manna <Manna 1971> who use a resolution theorem prover to compute the program which performs a completely specified input-output transformation. The difficulties of describing the IO properties of a complex program are thus compounded by the lack of expressivity of predicate calculus and the general lack of directedness of theorem provers.

6. In <Winston 1970> Patrick Winston describes a system for learning structural descriptions of Blocks World scenes by abstraction

from a carefully chosen training sequence. These descriptions are suitable for recognition by model-matching. In his work Winston makes use of the idea of a "near-miss", an example which differs from the concept being learned in only one essential way. This is closely related to the idea of a simple bug in programming. That is, a bug which is due to only one underlying cause. Indeed, both HACKER and people find more complex bugs difficult if not impossible to debug.

7. CONNIVER <McDermott 1972>, a descendent of PLANNER <Hewitt 1972> used for the implementation of HACKER, supports a pattern-directed data base with pattern-directed procedure invocation.

8. Pattern matching is a well known "bag of worms" in computer science. Numerous languages have been devised to formalize the ideas involved, including SNOBOL <Farber 1964> and CONVERT <Guzman 1966>. Recently, the introduction of pattern-directed data retrieval and especially pattern-directed procedure invocation by PLANNER <Hewitt 1972> and its descendants -- MICRO-PLANNER <Sussman 1970>, CONNIVER <McDermott 1972>, and QA4 <Rulifson 1971,1972> -- have further complicated the issues and the associated syntax.

9. PLANNER <Hewitt 1972> is Carl Hewitt's language for problem solving. It has raised many important issues and the resulting controversies have caused it to spawn a slew of descendants. CONNIVER <McDermott 1972> is a descendant of PLANNER which is the result of arguments against the Automatic Backtrack Control Structure espoused by PLANNER. The arguments are documented in <Sussman 1972>. HACKER and the code he manipulates are written in CONNIVER.

10. IF-ADDED methods are the CONNIVER <McDermott 1972> equivalent of PLANNER <Hewitt 1972> Antecedent Theorems. They monitor all items (assertions) added to the pattern-directed data-base. If an item is added which matches the invocation pattern of some IF-ADDED method, the process is interrupted and the body of the method is executed. Such data-base monitors are useful for maintaining the consistency of the data-base by making related changes or watching out for

specific problems when something is added.

11. CONNIVER <McDermott 1972> has a generalized control structure featuring a list-structure control stack built from objects called control frames. The user can (and is encouraged to) access, retain, and manipulate the control structure. He can evaluate expressions with respect to a selected control environment, or he can continue, go to, or exit from such an environment. Thus the user can easily construct such control mechanisms as multiprocessing, time-sharing (with interrupts), and backtracking. Bobrow and Wegbreit <Bobrow 1972> have proposed an efficient means of implementing such stack retention schemes.

12. The FINDSPACE Problem is a perceptual problem encountered by Blocks World problem solvers. The problem is how to determine if there is space on a surface for an object, and if so, where. Though at one level it is an elementary analytic geometry problem, it quickly involves such difficult questions as how to describe space and constraints on space so that they can be manipulated on a symbolic level. The name "the FINDSPACE problem" originates in Terry Winograd's system <Winograd 1971> as the name of his function which performs the required geometric manipulations. Scott Fahlman has given thought to this problem -- see <Fahlman 1973>. Gregory Pfister has an excellent algorithm for the numerical processing involved (personal communication).

13. MACLISP <White 1970>, <Moon 1974> is a powerful version of LISP <McCarthy 1965> developed at the MIT Artificial Intelligence Laboratory and MIT Project MAC. It is noted for its extremely efficient implementation, often at the expense of its error-handling system.

14. CONNIVER <McDermott 1972> supports a data-base mechanism in which the user may construct a tree of world-models in which each node corresponds to an incremental change from the model of its parent node. This structure is useful for doing hypothetical reasoning and modeling time. Drew V. McDermott <McDermott 1973> has made extensive use of this mechanism in his plausible inference system.

15. This operation, COMBINE, was originally described by Reynolds <Reynolds 1970> and Plotkin <Plotkin 1970>. The set of patterns are partially ordered by substitution instance. The resulting lattice has the standard operations "meet" and "join" defined on it. Meet corresponds to the "most general common instance" -- the UNIFY operation of resolution theorem proving. The join operation is the "most specific common generalization" -- the COMBINE operation used by the HACKER generalizer.

16. LOGO Turtle Geometry is an exciting new approach to teaching of mathematical concepts to children (see <Papert 1972a,b>). In this approach, the children are taught to program a computer to control a small robot (called a "Turtle") which can draw patterns by dragging a pen. Ira Goldstein has been designing a system which will debug elementary LOGO Turtle Programs. See <Goldstein 1973> for more details.

17. ITS is the time-sharing system for a Digital Equipment Corp. PDP-10 which was designed for use by the MIT-AI laboratory. It includes various powerful features which are described in <Eastlake 1972>. One of these features, the MAR interrupt, is essentially the time-shared equivalent of the machine's address stop switch. A user may, if he so desires, receive an interrupt on read, write, or execute of any selected memory register.

18. Fahlman's <Fahlman 1973> program [Note 3] does not share this prejudice. Part of the expertise of his program is knowing what to do when something goes wrong.

19. In Greenblatt's Chess Program <Greenblatt 1967>, every board position investigated (in a given game) is remembered in a hash table and associated with its backed-up score. Thus, a position need only be searched out once in any particular game. Samuel's Checkers Program <Samuel 1959> actually improved significantly over time by using this kind of rote learning technique from game to game. Samuel's program also attempted to do some "generalization learning" in which modifications were made to the board evaluation polynomial. Two such methods were tried. In one, the coefficients of the polynomial were changed, and in another, various terms in the polynomial were replaced.

20. The STRIPS problem solver <Fikes 1972> has an experimental
    system for assimilating and using generalized (variabilized)
    robot plans produced during its normal problem-solving
    activity.

Bibliography

<Balzer 1972>
Balzer, Robert
Automatic Programming
USC-ISI Technical Memo 1 (September 1972)

<Bobrow 1972>
Bobrow, D.G. and B. Wegbreit
A Model and Stack Implementation of Multiple Environments
Bolt, Beranek, and Newman Inc. Report No.2334 (1972)

<Bogen 1973>
Bogen, R. et al
MACSYMA User's Manual
M.I.T. Project MAC (February 1973)

<Buchanan 1969>
Buchanan, B.G., G.L. Sutherland, and E.A. Feigenbaum
"HEURISTIC DENDRAL: A Program for Generating Explanatory
Hypotheses in Organic Chemistry"
in <MI4>

<Eastlake 1972>
Eastlake, Donald E.
ITS Status Report
AI Memo 238 MIT-AI Laboratory (April 1972)

<Fahlman 1973>
Fahlman, Scott
A Planning System For Robot Construction Tasks
Master's Thesis (February 1973) MIT-AI-Laboratory

128

<Farber 1964>
Farber, D.J., R.E. Griswold, and I.P. Polonsky
"SNOBOL, A String Manipulation Language"
JACM Vol.11, No.2 (January 1964)

<Fikes 1972>
Fikes, Richard E., Peter E. Hart, and Nils J. Nilsson
"Learning and Executing Generalized Robot Plans"
Artificial Intelligence 3 (1972), pp.251-288

<Goldstein 1973>
Goldstein, Ira
An Intelligent Monitor for LOGO
PhD Thesis (August 1973)
MIT-AI-Laboratory

<Green 1969 a>
Green, C.
"Theorem Proving by Resolution as a Basis for Question-Answering
Systems"
in <MI4>

<Green 1969 b>
Green, C.
The Application of Theorem-Proving to Question-Answering Systems
PhD Thesis (1969)
Stanford University

<Greenblatt 1967>
Greenblatt, R. et al
"The Greenblatt Chess Program"
Proc. FJCC (1967) pp.801-810
also AI-Memo 174, MIT-AI Laboratory (1969)

<Guzman 1966>
Guzman, Adolpho and H.V. McIntosh
CONVERT
CACM (August 1966)

<Hewitt 1972>
Hewitt, C.
Description and Theoretical Analysis (Using Schemata) of PLANNER: A Language for Proving Theorems and Manipulating Models in a Robot
PhD Thesis (June 1971)
AI-TR-258 MIT-AI-Laboratory (April 1972)

<Hewitt 1971>
Hewitt, C.
"Procedural Embedding of Knowledge in PLANNER"
Proc. IJCAI 2 (September 1971)

<Manna 1971>
Manna, Z. and R.J. Waldinger
"Toward Automatic Program Synthesis"
CACM (March 1971)

<McCarthy 1965>
McCarthy et al
LISP 1.5 Programmer's Manual
MIT Press (1965, 1966)

<McDermott 1972>
McCermott, D.V. and G.J. Sussman
The CONNIVER Reference Manual
AI Memo 259 MIT-AI Laboratory (May 1972) (Revised July 1973)

<McDermott 1973>
McDermott, D.V.
Assimilation of New Information by a Natural Language Understanding System
Master's Thesis (February 1973)
MIT-AI Laboratory

<MI4>
Machine Intelligence 4
Meltzer, B. and D. Michie (eds.)
Edinburgh University Press (1969)

<MI5>
Machine Intelligence 5
Meltzer, B. and D. Michie (eds.)
American Elsevier Publishing Co. (1970)

<Minsky 1965>
Minsky, M.L.
"Matter, Mind, and Models"
IFIP (1965)

<Minsky 1966>
Minsky, M.L.
"Why Programming is a Good Medium for Expressing Poorly
Understood and Sloppily Formulated Ideas"
Design and Planning (1966)

<Minsky 1970>
Minsky, M.L.
"Form and Content in Computer Science"
JACM (April 1970)

<Minsky 1972>
Minsky, M.L.
Progress Report
AI Memo 252, MIT AI Laboratory (January 1972)

<Moon 1974>
Moon, David A.
MACLISP Reference Manual
MIT Project MAC (April 1974)

<Newell 1959>
Newell, A., J.C. Shaw, and H.A. Simon
"Report on a General Problem-Solving Program"
in *Proceedings of the International Conference on Information
Processing*
Paris:UNESCO House (1959)

<Newell 1972>
Newell, Allen, and Herbert A. Simon
Human Problem Solving
Prentice-Hall Inc. (1972)

<Papert 1972a>
Papert, Seymour A.
"Teaching Children Thinking"
Programmed Learning and Educational Technology, Vol.9, No.5
(September 1972)

<Papert 1972b>
Papert, S.A.
"On Making a Theorem for a Child"
Proc. ACM Conference (August 1972)

<Plotkin 1970>
Plotkin, G.D.
"A Note on Inductive Generalization"
in <MI5>

<Reynolds 1970>
Reynolds, J.C.
"Transformational Systems and the Algebraic Structure of Atomic
Formulas"
in <MI5>

<Rulifson 1971>
Rulifson, J.F.
QA4 Programming Concepts
Stanford AI Technical Note 60 (August 1971)

<Rulifson 1972>
Rulifson, J.F.
"The QA4 Language Applied to Robot Planning"
FJCC (1972)

<Samuel 1959>
Samuel, A.L.
"Some Studies in Machine Learning Using the Game of Checkers"
IBM Journal of Research and Development (1959)
also in Feldman and Feigenbaum (eds.)
Computers and Thought (1963)

<Sussman 1970>
Sussman, G.J., T. Winograd, and E. Charniak
Micro-Planner Reference Manual
AI Memo 203, MIT-AI Laboratory (July 1970)
(revised December 1971)

<Sussman 1972>
Sussman, G.J. and D.V. McDermott
"From PLANNER to CONNIVER - A Genetic Approach"
F JCC (1972)

<White 1970>
White, J.L.
Interim LISP Progress Report
AI Memo 190, MIT Project MAC (March 1970)

<Winograd 1971>
Winograd, T.
Procedures as a Representation for Data in a Computer Program for Understanding Natural Language
PhD Thesis (August 1970)
and
AI-TR-17 (MAC-TR-84)
MIT AI Laboratory (February 1971)

<Winston 1970>
Winston, P.H.
Learning Structural Descriptions from Examples
PhD Thesis (January 1970)
also MAC-TR-76 MIT AI Laboratory (September 1970)